MathSmart in 90 Days 3

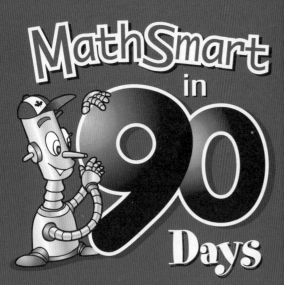

Contents

Numbers to 100 (1)

Fill in the blanks to match the number of stickers in each group.

①

_____ = 6 tens + _____ ones

= _____ + _____

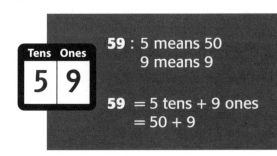

Tens	Ones
5	9

59 : 5 means 50
9 means 9

59 = 5 tens + 9 ones
= 50 + 9

②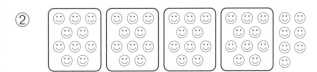

_____ = _____ tens + _____ ones

= _____ + _____

③

_____ = _____ tens + _____ ones

= _____ + _____

Write the 2-digit numbers or the meanings of the digits.

④  : 4 means 40
2 means 2

⑤ : 8 means 80
4 means 4

⑥  : 5 means 50
1 means 1

⑦ : 2 means 20
6 means 6

⑧ 73 : 7 means _____
3 means _____

⑨ 97 : 9 means _____
7 means _____

Fill in the missing numbers.

⑩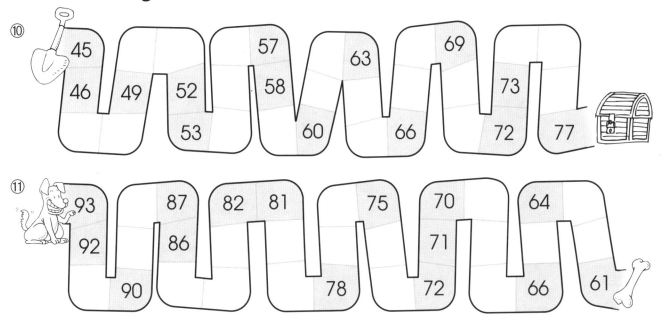

45 46 49 52 53 57 58 60 63 66 69 72 73 77

⑪

93 92 90 87 86 82 81 78 75 72 71 70 66 64 61

Connect the dots by skip-counting.

⑫ Count by 5's. Start from 10.

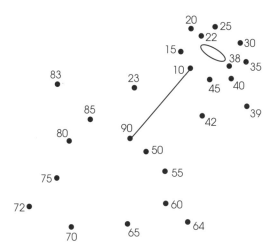

⑬ Count by 10's. Start from 10.

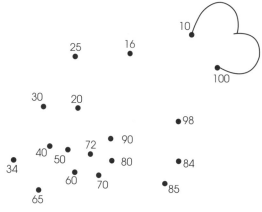

⑭ Count by 2's. Start from 26.

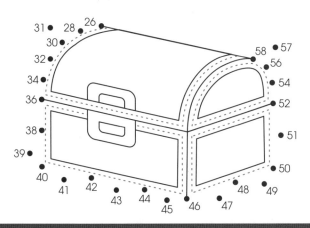

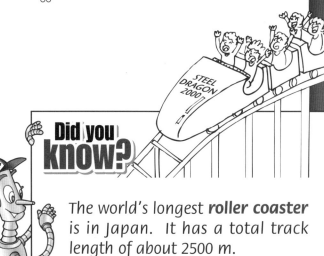

Did you know?

The world's longest **roller coaster** is in Japan. It has a total track length of about 2500 m.

Day
2

Numbers to 100 (2)

A table for twenty-five, please.

K & R Restaurant

Circle the greater number in each pair.

① | 39 | 25 |

② | 64 | 19 |

③ | 42 | 53 |

④ | 30 | 36 |

Put the numbers in order from greatest to least. Then locate them on the number line.

Comparing 2-digit numbers:

1st Compare the digits in the tens place. If they are the same, go to the next step.

2nd Compare the digits in the ones place.

e.g.   46   49

Compare   **4**6 **4**9   the same

Compare   4**6** 4**9**   9 is greater.

49 is greater than 46.

⑤   36, 52, 40, 39

52, _____ ;

52

30   40   50

⑥   88, 98, 90, 83

_____ ;

80   90   100

⑦   72, 45, 66, 53

_____ ;

40   50   60   70

⑧   28, 19, 33, 54

_____ ;

10   20   30   40   50   60

Ten	10
Twenty	20
Thirty	30
Forty	40
Fifty	50
Sixty	60
Seventy	70
Eighty	80
Ninety	90
Hundred	100

Write the numbers in numerals.

⑨ Twenty-five _____   ⑩ Forty-nine _____

⑪ Thirty-six _____   ⑫ Fifty-four _____

⑬ Seventy-one _____   ⑭ Eighty-two _____

⑮ Sixty-seven _____   ⑯ Ninety-four _____

⑰ Thirty-eight _____   ⑱ Sixty-three _____

⑲ Forty-three _____   ⑳ Seventy-six _____

Write the numbers in words.

㉑ 46 _____   ㉒ 59 _____

㉓ 83 _____   ㉔ 94 _____

㉕ 62 _____   ㉖ 37 _____

㉗ 75 _____   ㉘ 21 _____

Find the numbers. Write the answers on the beads of the necklace.

㉙ Ⓐ 2 more than 28   Ⓑ one more than seventy-three

Ⓒ 2 less than 31   Ⓓ two less than ninety-seven

Ⓔ 1 more than 24

Ⓕ one less than fifty-one

The **Vancouver Island Marmot** is a unique Canadian species found only on Vancouver Island in British Columbia. Sadly, their population is estimated to be just over 100.

Day 3 Ordinal Numbers

The 56th duck is the cutest.

Write the ordinal numbers in 2 ways.

① twenty-fifth _____ th

② seventy-sixth _____

③ fifty-first _____

④ thirty-third _____

⑤ eighty-fourth _____

⑥ ninety-eighth _____

10th	tenth	20th	twentieth
30th	thirtieth	40th	fortieth
50th	fiftieth	60th	sixtieth
70th	seventieth	80th	eightieth
90th	ninetieth		
100th	one hundredth		

⑦ 40th _____

⑨ 73rd _____

⑪ 42nd _____

⑧ 69th _____

⑩ 80th _____

⑫ 91st _____

Draw a line to help Dickie Duck find his towel. Start from the 52nd dot.

⑬

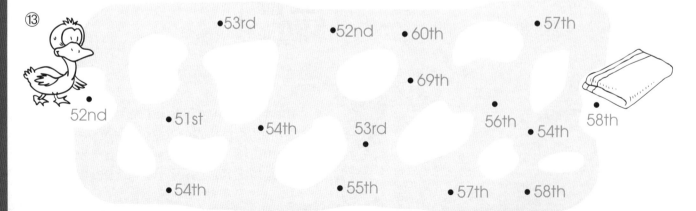

•53rd   •52nd   •60th   •57th

•69th

52nd   •51st   •54th   53rd   56th   •54th   58th

•54th   •55th   •57th   •58th

Fill in the ordinal numbers. Then solve the problems.

⑭ a.

b. How many balloons are there between the 36th and 42nd balloon?   _____ balloons

c. If Alex ties one big balloon after the 42nd balloon, what will the position of the big balloon be?   _____

d. If Joe removes the 37th balloon, what will be the new position of the balloon with a star?   _____

⑮

Join our

_____ Anniversary Party

Date: Sept _____

*   Every _____ guest will

get a special  .

Today is the twenty-sixth of September. We will have a party to celebrate our fifty-fourth anniversary tomorrow. Every tenth guest will get a special gift.

⑯

Look at my diamond ring. It is for our seventy-fifth wedding anniversary.

For the _____ anniversary

Did you know?

Paul Martin is the 21st Prime Minister of Canada.

DATE:

Addition of 2-Digit Numbers

Do the addition.

①
```
   32
+  17
```

②
```
   25
+  39
```

③
```
   18
+  48
```

④
```
   54
+  37
```

⑤ 29 + 16 = _____

⑥ 44 + 23 = _____

⑦ 38 + 49 = _____

⑧ 31 + 8 = _____

⑨ 9 + 65 = _____

⑩ 19 + 54 = _____

⑪ 43 + 28 = _____

⑫ 29 + 35 = _____

⑬ 51 + 42 = _____

The balls with the correct answers belong to Eva. Help her do the addition and colour her balls.

⑭

16 + 25	26 + 47
32 + 17	33 + 59
40 + 6	24 + 18
25 + 13	39 + 46
64 + 8	13 + 68
35 + 25	7 + 73

 73
 41
 62
 38
85

 42
 92
 72
 28
 81

 49
 31
 46

 60
70
 80

Look at the pictures. Solve the problems.

⑮

a. How many candies are there in the jar and the bag in all?

_____ = _____

_____ candies

b. How many candies are there in two bags?

_____ = _____   _____ candies

c. How many candies are there in two jars?

_____ = _____   _____ candies

⑯ **Group A**

15

24

Group B

26

17

a. How many boys are there in the two groups?

_____ = _____

_____ boys

b. How many girls are there in the two groups?

_____ = _____

_____ girls

c. How many children are there in Group A?

_____ = _____

_____ children

d. How many children are there in Group B?

_____ = _____   _____ children

e. How many children are there in all?

_____ = _____   _____ children

Day
5

Subtraction of 2-Digit Numbers

Pieces of
chocolate left:

$$\begin{array}{r} \overset{2\ \ 10}{\cancel{3}\ \cancel{0}} \\ -1\ 4 \\ \hline 1\ 6 \end{array}$$

Do the subtraction.

①
$$\begin{array}{r} 2\ 5 \\ -\ 1\ 7 \\ \hline \end{array}$$

②
$$\begin{array}{r} 5\ 6 \\ -\ 2\ 8 \\ \hline \end{array}$$

③
$$\begin{array}{r} 6\ 0 \\ -\ 4\ 1 \\ \hline \end{array}$$

$$\begin{array}{r} \overset{3\ \ 12}{4\ \cancel{2}} \\ -1\ 9 \\ \hline 2\ 3 \end{array}$$
 ← Borrow 1 from the tens.
1 ten + 2 ones
= 12

④ 37 – 23 = _____

⑤ 62 – 4 = _____

⑥ 50 – 24 = _____

⑦ 44 – 25 = _____

⑧ 67 – 8 = _____

⑨ 39 – 22 = _____

⑩ 56 – 48 = _____

⑪ 75 – 36 = _____

⑫ 91 – 78 = _____

Choose the correct number to make each subtraction sentence correct.

⑬
| 29 |
| 19 |
| 39 |

37 – _____ = 18

50 – _____ = 11

⑭
| 26 |
| 16 |
| 36 |

42 – _____ = 16

64 – _____ = 28

⑮
| 71 |
| 91 |
| 81 |

_____ – 54 = 27

_____ – 38 = 33

⑯
| 55 |
| 65 |
| 45 |

_____ – 26 = 39

_____ – 7 = 38

Look at Sonia's cards. Help her solve the problems.

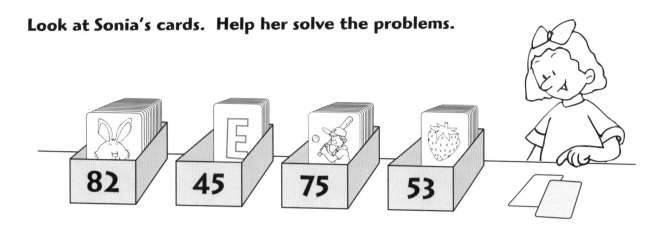

⑰ If Sonia gives 17 animal cards to her friends, how many animal cards will be left?

_____ animal cards

⑱ How many more baseball cards than letter cards does Sonia have?

_____ more

⑲ How many fewer letter cards than fruit cards does Sonia have?

_____ fewer

⑳ If Kevin has 80 baseball cards, how many more baseball cards does he have than Sonia?

_____ more

㉑ If Kevin gives 9 baseball cards to Sonia, how many cards will he have left?

_____ cards

Day 6

Addition and Subtraction of 2-Digit Numbers

Total number of 🎄:
36 + 48 = 84

Number of 🎄 left:

$$\begin{array}{r} {\scriptstyle 7\ 14} \\ 8\,4 \\ -5 \\ \hline 7\,9 \end{array}$$

The Christmas ornaments with the matching answers belong to Amanda. Find the answers and write the letters to complete what Amanda says.

 A 90

① 42 – 29 = _____   ② 32 + 59 = _____

③ 27 + 54 = _____   ④ 56 + 12 = _____   **B** 91

⑤ 46 + 18 = _____   ⑥ 70 – 22 = _____

⑦ 63 + 12 = _____   ⑧ 92 – 47 = _____    **C** 46

⑨ 9 + 49 = _____   ⑩ 87 – 55 = _____

⑪ 90 – 68 = _____   ⑫ 45 + 47 = _____    **D** 45

⑬ 59 + 12 = _____   ⑭ 83 – 26 = _____

⑮ 71 – 55 = _____   ⑯ 48 + 3 = _____    **E** 64

⑰ 89 – 79 = _____   ⑱ 8 + 45 = _____

 **F** 16

⑲ _____ , and _____ are mine!

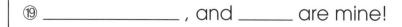

Solve the problems.

⑳ Joseph has 56 pencils and Lily has 37.

    a. How many pencils do Joseph and Lily have in all?

       _____ pencils

    b. How many more pencils does Joseph have than Lily?

       _____ more

㉑ There are 64 big fish and 35 small fish.

    a. How many more big fish than small fish are there?

       _____ more

    b. How many fish are there in all?

       _____ fish

㉒ Aunt Jenny has 18 boxes of juice left after giving 35 boxes to the children. How many boxes of juice did Aunt Jenny have at first?

_____ boxes of juice

More than 2500 people grow **Christmas trees** in Nova Scotia and each year nearly 2 million trees are sent to the market.

Day 7

Numbers to 1000

326 = 3 hundreds 2 tens 6 ones

Fill in the blanks for each group of pictures.

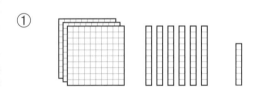

⬛ = 100 | = 10   ▫ = 1

Hundreds	Tens	Ones
2	4	5

2 means 2 hundreds or 200;
4 means 4 tens or 40; and
5 means 5 ones or 5.

①

_____ hundreds _____ tens _____ ones = _____

②

_____ hundreds _____ tens _____ ones

= _____

③

_____ hundreds _____ tens _____ ones

= _____

Write the meanings of the digits.

④ 398

3 means _____

9 means _____

8 means _____

⑤ 572

5 means _____

7 means _____

2 means _____

⑥ 863

8 means _____

6 means _____

3 means _____

Fill in the missing numbers.

⑦ 327   328   329   _____   _____   332   _____   334

⑧ 849   850   _____   852   _____   _____   855   856

⑨ 795   796   _____   _____   799   _____   801   802

⑩ 468   469   _____   _____   472   473   _____   475

Answer the questions.

⑪ What number is 1 more than 599?   _____

⑫ What number is 2 less than 461?   _____

⑬ How many numbers are there between 364 and 372?   _____

⑭ Write two 3-digit numbers that are greater than 620.   _____

Read the clues to find the 3-digit numbers to complete the puzzle.

⑮

Across

A. 3 hundreds 6 ones
B. 2 less than 421
C. 100 more than 200

Down

1. between 373 and 375
2. 9 hundreds 3 tens
3. 4 hundreds

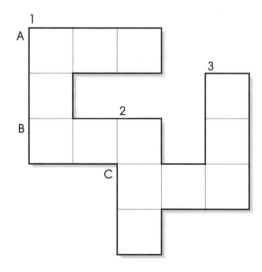

Did you know?

Bill Gates, who was born on October 28, 1955, was the richest man in the world in 2005.

DATE:

Counting by 10's or 25's

..., 100, 125, 150, 175, 200, ...

..., 100, 110, 120, 130, 140, 150, ...

Fill in the missing numbers.

①

450	460					510		530

		590				550	

②

25		125					400	
50			175	250	275		375	

③

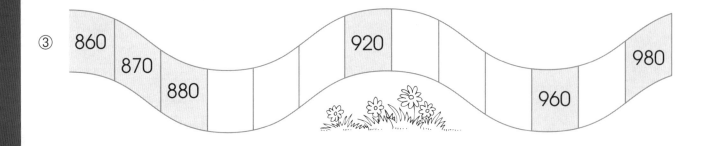

860, 870, 880, ___, ___, 920, ___, ___, 960, ___, 980

④

770		580			620		650
760	750			710		680	660

Connect the dots by skip-counting.

⑤ Count by 10's. Start from 500.

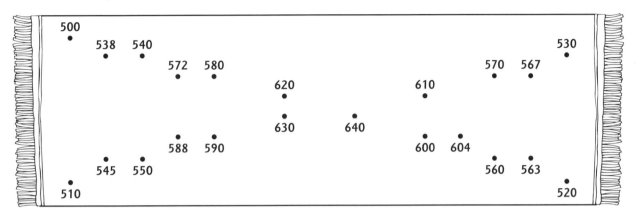

⑥ Count by 25's. Start from 25.

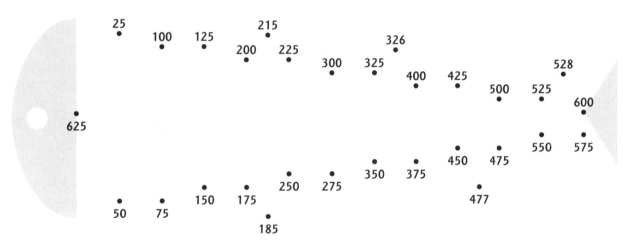

Colour every ten hearts in a different colour and circle every twenty-five hearts. Then circle the correct answer.

⑦ Which is a faster way to count?

By 10's   By 25's

Day
9

Counting by 50's or 100's

100, 200, 300, 400

50, 100, 150,
200, 250, 300,
350, 400

Fill in the missing numbers.

①	450	500	550	_____	_____	700	
②	200	300	_____	_____	_____	700	
③	150	200	_____	_____	350	_____	
④	400	500	_____	_____	800	_____	
⑤	650	700	_____	_____	850	_____	

When you count by 50's, the digit in the ones place of the numbers must be 0.

e.g.   25**0**, 40**0**

When you count by 100's, the numbers that you get must have 0 in the ones and tens places.

e.g.   5**00**, 7**00**

Count the stickers by 50's or 100's. Write the numbers.

50	50	50	50	50

⑥   Count by 50's.

_____

_____

50	50	50	50	50

⑦   Count by 100's.

_____

The child who reaches the hoola hoop first is the winner.
Draw lines in different colours to show the paths of
the children. Then answer the questions.

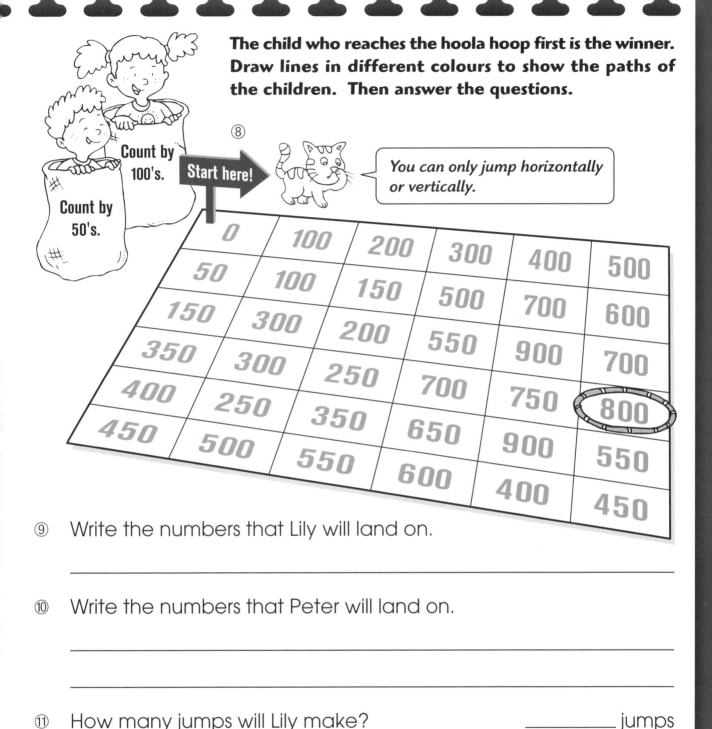

Count by 100's.

Count by 50's.

Start here!

⑧

You can only jump horizontally or vertically.

0	100	200	300	400	500
50	100	150	500	700	600
150	300	200	550	900	700
350	300	250	700	900	700
400	250	350	700	750	800
450	500	550	650	900	550
			600	400	450

⑨   Write the numbers that Lily will land on.

_____

⑩   Write the numbers that Peter will land on.

_____

_____

⑪   How many jumps will Lily make?   _____ jumps

⑫   How many jumps will Peter make?   _____ jumps

⑬   Who will be the winner?

_____

⑭   If the hoola hoop is on 750,
       will Lily be the winner?

_____

Did you know?

There are 50 **pennies** in a
roll. A roll of pennies is
worth 50¢.

Penny

DATE: _____

Day 10 Addition of 3-Digit Numbers (1)

Yummy Cookies

```
  1 6 8
+   3 0
-------
  1 9 8
```

Hot Deal!

Buy 168 🍪 and get 30 Free!

Good deal!

198

Do the addition.

①
```
  3 2 4
+ 1 1 3
```

②
```
  2 1 6
+ 5 3 1
```

③
```
  1 1 7
+ 4 8 0
```

④
```
  4 6 2
+   1 5
```

⑤
```
  7 4 4
+ 1 1 0
```

⑥
```
    5 9
+ 2 3 0
```

⑦
```
    7 5
+ 2 0 4
```

⑧
```
  2 7 2
+ 1 1 5
```

⑨
```
  3 1 6
+ 3 7 2
```

Adding 3-digit numbers:

1st Add the ones.

2nd Add the tens.

3rd Add the hundreds.

e.g.

```
    3rd 2nd 1st
  4   0   5
+ 1   3   4
-----------
  5   3   9
```

405 + 134 = 539

Find out how many cookies are in each box. Then colour the box with the most cookies.

⑩ 423 + 104 = [   ]

⑪ 336 + 41 = [   ]

⑫ 224 + 414 = [   ]

⑬ 56 + 612 = [   ]

⑭ 552 + 131 = [   ]

⑮ 481 + 18 = [   ]

Solve the problems.

⑯ Judy has 415 heart stickers and 74 star stickers. How many stickers does Judy have in all?

_____ = _____   _____ stickers

⑰ There are 130 crayons in a box. If Sonia has 2 boxes of crayons, how many crayons does Sonia have in all?

_____ = _____   _____ crayons

⑱ Ted has 245 pennies. If Ted's sister has 42 more pennies than Ted, how many pennies does Ted's sister have?

_____ = _____   _____ pennies

⑲ Aunt Jenny has bought 327 chocolate eggs. If Aunt Jenny buys 60 more, how many chocolate eggs will she have in all?

_____ = _____   _____ chocolate eggs

⑳ Louis has 14 chocolate cookies and 134 almond cookies.

a. How many cookies does Louis have in all?

_____ cookies

b. If Eva has 30 more cookies than Louis, how many cookies does Eva have?

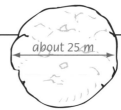

_____ cookies

Did you know?

about 25 m

The largest **cookie** was made by a cookie factory in New Zealand in 1996. It had an area of 487 square metres!

Day
11

Addition of 3-Digit Numbers (2)

125 ❀

188 ❀

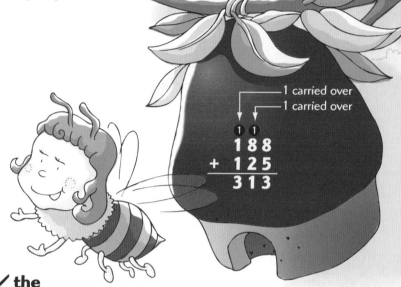

1 carried over
1 carried over

```
  ① ①
   1 8 8
 + 1 2 5
 ───────
   3 1 3
```

Do the addition. Then check ✔ the addition with the greatest answer in each group.

①

Ⓐ
```
   3 6 1
 + 1 1 9
```

Ⓑ 65 + 408 = _____

Ⓒ 226 + 187 = _____

②

Ⓐ
```
   7 5 4
 +   8 8
```

Ⓑ 588 + 163 = _____

Ⓒ 705 + 196 = _____

③

Ⓐ
```
   1 8 7
 + 1 8 7
```

Ⓑ 353 + 68 = _____

Ⓒ 284 + 155 = _____

④

Ⓐ
```
   2 0 9
 + 7 1 6
```

Ⓑ 474 + 507 = _____

Ⓒ 622 + 299 = _____

Remember to carry groups of 10 to the column on the left.

e.g. 465 + 198 = _____

1st Add the ones.

```
     1
   4 6 5
 + 1 9 8
 ───────
       3
```
5 + 8 = 13, carry 1 to the tens.

2nd Add the tens.

```
   1 1
   4 6 5
 + 1 9 8
 ───────
     6 3
```
1 + 6 + 9 = 16, carry 1 to the hundreds.

3rd Add the hundreds.

```
   1 1
   4 6 5
 + 1 9 8
 ───────
   6 6 3
```
1 + 4 + 1 = 6

465 + 198 = 663

Solve the problems.

⑤ There are 427 red roses and 365 pink roses. How many roses are there in all?

_____ roses

⑥ Aunt Polly has 108 big sunflowers and 56 small sunflowers in her backyard. How many sunflowers does Aunt Polly have in all?

_____ sunflowers

⑦ Lisa has 137 animal stickers. If she has 94 more flower stickers than animal stickers, how many flower stickers does Lisa have?

_____ flower stickers

⑧ Mr. Jenkins bought 73 carnations and 288 roses.

   a. How many flowers did Mr. Jenkins buy in all?

      _____ flowers

   b. If Mrs. Brown bought 66 more flowers than Mr. Jenkins, how many flowers did Mrs. Brown buy in all?

_____ flowers

Did you know?

Bumblebees form colonies like honeybees but their hives are much smaller. They usually live in colonies of 30 to 400.

Subtraction of 3-Digit Numbers (1)

487
– 135
_____
352

487 ●

135

Peter's favourite fruit is the one with the greatest answer. Do the subtraction and complete what Peter says.

① 384
– 165

② 596
– 283

③ 750
– 138

④ 862
– 47

⑤ 455
– 263

⑥ 643
– 317

⑦ 539 – 460 = _____

⑧ 482 – 331 = _____

⑨ 384 – 59 = _____

⑩ 763 – 258 = _____

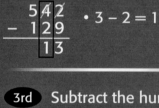

Subtracting 3-digit numbers:

e.g. 542 – 129

1st Subtract the ones.

3 12
5 4̶ 2̶
– 1 2 9
_____
3

• 2 is not big enough to subtract 9.
• Borrow 1 from the tens.
• 12 – 9 = 3

2nd Subtract the tens.

3 12
5 4̶ 2̶
– 1 2 9
_____
1 3

• 3 – 2 = 1

3rd Subtract the hundreds.

3 12
5 4̶ 2̶
– 1 2 9
_____
4 1 3

• 5 – 1 = 4

542 – 129 = 413

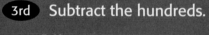

My favourite fruit is
⑪ _____

See how many cups of juice were sold last week.
Help the shopowner, Mr. Miller, solve the problems.

Number of Cups of Juice Sold Last Week			
865 cups	463 cups	659 cups	523 cups

Special
of the Month

⑫ How many more cups of orange juice than pineapple juice were sold?

_____ = _____

_____ more

⑬ How many fewer cups of orange juice than strawberry juice were sold?

_____ = _____   _____ fewer

⑭ How many fewer cups of apple juice than pineapple juice were sold?

_____ = _____   _____ fewer

⑮ If 338 cups of orange juice were sold on the weekdays, how many cups of orange juice were sold on the weekend?

_____ = _____   _____ cups

⑯ What was the difference between the most cups of juice sold and the fewest?

_____ = _____   _____ cups

⑰ Which juice above was the most popular? Why?

_____

Day
13

Subtraction of 3-Digit Numbers (2)

Number of 🧁 left:

```
  4 9 10
  5 0 0
- 3 2 4
  1 7 6
```

176
500

Do the subtraction.

①
```
  3 7 5
- 1 8 6
```

②
```
  7 8 2
- 1 9 7
```

③
```
  8 6 3
- 4 7 9
```

④
```
  4 0 0
- 2 6 5
```

⑤
```
  3 9 2
-   9 4
```

⑥
```
  5 7 7
- 2 9 9
```

> Subtracting 3-digit numbers:
> - Subtract the ones.
> - Subtract the tens.
> - Subtract the hundreds.
>
> If you cannot subtract, borrow 10 from the column on the left.
>
> e.g. borrow borrow
> ```
>   3 10 15
>   4  1  5
> - 2  9  8
>   1  1  7
> ```

Match the subtraction sentences with the boxes that have the same answer.

⑦ 324 – 168 = _____ •

953 – 586 = _____ •

804 – 385 = _____ •

597 – 198 = _____ •

• 828 – 429 = _____

• 416 – 49 = _____

• 705 – 286 = _____

• 621 – 465 = _____

Solve the problems. Show your work in the spaces provided.

⑧ The number of chocolate cookies is 427 fewer than that of almond cookies. If there are 729 almond cookies, how many chocolate cookies are there?

_____ chocolate cookies

⑨ Aunt Christie has a box of 400 chocolate bars. If she takes 165 chocolate bars from the box, how many chocolate bars will be left?

_____ chocolate bars

⑩ Sonia has 108 pencils. If she gives 39 pencils to her sisters, how many pencils will she have left?

_____ pencils

⑪ Jane has 322 ribbons. If she uses 159 ribbons to make crafts, how many ribbons will be left?

_____ ribbons

A **chocolate chip muffin** has about 27 g of fat, which is $\frac{3}{7}$ of the total 560 calories.

DATE: _____

Addition and Subtraction of 3-Digit Numbers

We have 381 🌰 in all, but I've picked 57 🌰 more than you.

$$\begin{array}{r} 162 \\ + 219 \\ \hline 381 \end{array} \qquad \begin{array}{r} 219 \\ - 162 \\ \hline 57 \end{array}$$

Find the answers.

① $\begin{array}{r} 125 \\ + 361 \\ \hline \end{array}$ ② $\begin{array}{r} 284 \\ + 406 \\ \hline \end{array}$ ③ $\begin{array}{r} 523 \\ - 297 \\ \hline \end{array}$ ④ $\begin{array}{r} 601 \\ - 378 \\ \hline \end{array}$

⑤ $168 + 274 = $ _____

⑥ $396 + 297 = $ _____

⑦ $205 - 89 = $ _____

⑧ $421 - 155 = $ _____

⑨ $751 - 188 = $ _____

⑩ $825 - 133 = $ _____

Follow the order of the answers to help Brother Squirrel find his acorn.

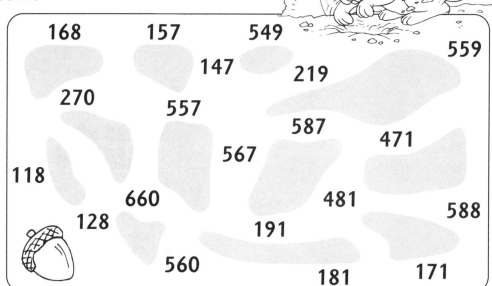

⑪ $384 + 165$

$261 - 114$

$860 - 273$

$175 + 306$

$339 - 148$

$257 + 403$

$716 - 588$

168   157   549   559
147   219
270   557
587   471
567
118
660   481   588
128   191
560   181   171

Solve the problems.

⑫ Uncle Louis spent 174 days collecting data for a project and 49 days organizing them. How many days in all did Uncle Louis spend on his project?

_____ = _____   _____ days

⑬ The total weight of robot A and robot B equals 752 blocks. If robot A weighs 298 blocks, how many blocks are needed to balance the weight of robot B?

_____ = _____   _____ blocks

⑭ Uncle Bill sold 287 ice cream cones on Saturday and 325 ice cream cones on Sunday. How many ice cream cones did Uncle Bill sell over the weekend?

_____ = _____   _____ ice cream cones

⑮ *I can see many children playing on the beach. There are 109 boys and 82 girls.*

a. How many children are there in all?

_____ = _____

_____ children

b. How many fewer girls than boys are there?

_____ = _____

_____ fewer

DATE: _____

Estimating Sums and Differences

		Sum	Difference
286	rounded up → 300	300	300
102	rounded down → 100	+ 100	− 100
		400	200

Round each number to the nearest hundred.

① 913 _____   ② 605 _____

③ 274 _____   ④ 896 _____

⑤ 570 _____   ⑥ 468 _____

⑦ 146 _____   ⑧ 593 _____

⑨ 217 _____   ⑩ 381 _____

⑪ 558 _____   ⑫ 664 _____

> **Rounding a 3-digit number to the nearest hundred:**
>
> e.g. 379 ← It is between 300 and 400.
>
> 379 (closer to 400)
>
> 300 ———————— 400
>
> 379 rounded to → 400
>
> **A number halfway between 2 numbers should be rounded up.**
>
> e.g. 350 rounded to → 400

Estimate by rounding each number to the nearest hundred. Then find the answers.

⑬
```
  359
+ 267
_____
```
Estimate _____

⑭
```
  544
+ 416
_____
```
Estimate _____

⑮
```
  827
- 459
_____
```
Estimate _____

⑯
```
  738
- 147
_____
```
Estimate _____

Estimate the answer for each question. Then calculate and colour the questions with answers greater than 500 to help Tony get to his toy.

⑰

A
$$425 + 295$$

B
$$924 - 187$$

C
$$800 - 653$$

D
$$381 - 258$$

E
$$336 + 392$$

F
$$911 - 746$$

G
$$203 + 214$$

H
$$654 - 126$$

I
$$556 - 382$$

J
$$466 - 312$$

K
$$359 - 124$$

L
$$857 - 208$$

M
$$189 + 713$$

Fill in the blanks to complete what the butterfly says.

⑱ There are 425 red flowers and 186 yellow flowers or about _____ flowers in all. If I've visited about 100 flowers, that means there are about _____ flowers I haven't visited yet.

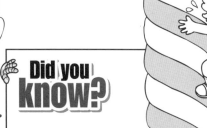

Did you know?

The world's largest **lollipop** was made in Sweden in 2003. It was as heavy as 70 Grade 3 students.

Relating Addition and Subtraction

396 + 258 = 654
258 + 396 = 654
654 − 396 = 258
654 − 258 = 396

Use the given number sentences to find the answers.

① 324 + 169 = 493

   493 − 324 = _____

② 514 + 178 = 692

   692 − 178 = _____

③ 500 − 281 = 219

   219 + 281 = _____

④ 925 − 430 = 495

   430 + 495 = _____

Write an addition and a subtraction sentence for each group of numbers.

⑤ (527)─(146)─(381)

   _____ + _____ = _____

   _____ − _____ = _____

⑥ (925)─(498)─(427)

   _____ + _____ = _____

   _____ − _____ = _____

⑦ (356)─(627)─(271)

   _____ + _____ = _____

   _____ − _____ = _____

⑧ (408)─(362)─(46)

   _____ + _____ = _____

   _____ − _____ = _____

Find the answers. Then match the number sentences that are related to each other by writing the correct letters in the circles.

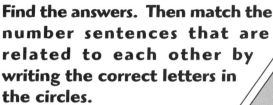

⑨

A 600 − 273 = _____

B 432 − 138 = _____

C 127 + 566 = _____

D 353 + 479 = _____

E 571 − 154 = _____

F 740 − 189 = _____

G 384 + 293 = _____

294 + 138 = _____ ◯

693 − 566 = _____ ◯

273 + 327 = _____ ◯

417 + 154 = _____ ◯

832 − 479 = _____ ◯

677 − 293 = _____ ◯

551 + 189 = _____ ◯

Solve the problems.

⑩ There are 653 red balls and 209 blue balls in a box, or a total of 862 balls. If Judy takes 209 balls from the box, there will be _____ balls left.

⑪ There are 427 apples in a tree. Joe picks 138 apples and 289 apples are left. If Joe picks the rest of the 289 apples, he will have picked _____ apples in all.

Fill in the missing numbers.

① 82 83 84 _____ _____ _____ 88 _____ _____ _____ 92

② 925 926 927 _____ _____ _____ _____ 932

③ 558 559 _____ _____ _____ 563 _____ 565

Fill in the correct numbers by skip-counting.

④ Count by 25's

25, _____ , _____ , _____ , _____ , _____ , _____

⑤ Count by 100's

300, _____ , _____ , _____ , _____ , _____ , _____

⑥ Count by 50's

650, _____ , _____ , _____ , _____ , _____ , _____

Find the answers.

⑦
$$\begin{array}{r} 95 \\ -\ 37 \\ \hline \end{array}$$

⑧
$$\begin{array}{r} 63 \\ +\ 28 \\ \hline \end{array}$$

⑨
$$\begin{array}{r} 275 \\ +\ 319 \\ \hline \end{array}$$

⑩
$$\begin{array}{r} 515 \\ -\ 478 \\ \hline \end{array}$$

⑪ 632 − 477 = _____   ⑫ 325 + 116 = _____

⑬ 524 − 189 = _____   ⑭ 128 + 128 = _____

⑮ 306 + 549 = _____   ⑯ 463 − 274 = _____

⑰ 500 − 332 = _____   ⑱ 710 + 98 = _____

Answer the questions. Write the answers in the balloon.

⑲ What number is 2 less than ninety-one? _____

⑳ What number is 1 more than 904? _____

㉑ What number is 100 less than 700? _____

㉒ Tom is standing behind the 80th child. What is Tom's position? _____

㉓ Tammy is standing in front of the fortieth child. What is Tammy's position? _____

Estimate the answers by rounding each number to the nearest hundred. Then find the exact answers.

㉔ There were 827 people attending the concert yesterday. If 329 of them were adults, how many children attended the concert?

_____ children

Estimate

㉕ A coffee shop sold 492 cups of coffee yesterday and 368 cups of coffee today. How many cups of coffee were sold in these two days?

_____ cups of coffee

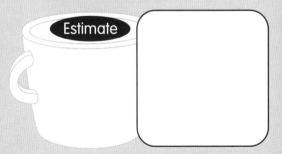
Estimate

㉖ Mrs. Sanders has baked 406 cookies. If she gives 157 cookies to her neighbours, how many cookies will be left?

_____ cookies

Estimate

DATE: _____

You Deserve A Break!

See how many vegetable sticks are in each group. Write the number in words.

① **10** _____

25 _____

50 _____

Fill the shapes with numbers while skip-counting each kind of vegetables. Then complete what the ant says.

② ⑩

Start counting from here.

Each group of the same kind of vegetable has the same number of sticks.

③ There are _____ broccoli sticks, _____ celery sticks, and _____ carrot sticks on the tray.

Answer the questions.

④ *There are 105 male ants and 98 female ants carrying the tray. How many ants are there in all?*

_____ ants

⑤ *If 163 ants have weapons, how many ants are without weapons?*

_____ ants

Write the ordinal numbers to complete what the ants say.

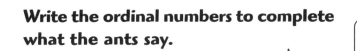

Hi! I'm David. I'm the 57th ant in line.

⑥ I'm the _____ .

⑦ I'm the _____ .

⑧ If I march more slowly, I will go behind David. I'll be the _____ in line.

Solve the problems.

⑨
```
  364
+ 472
```

⑩
```
  500
- 276
```

⑪
```
  829
- 734
```

⑫
```
  405
+ 269
```

Day
19

Checking Subtraction by Using Addition

Check
```
  175
+ 325
  500
```

```
  500
- 325
  175
```

Help Robert check his answers by using addition. Put a check mark ✔ in the circle if his answer is correct; otherwise, put a cross ✗.

You can use addition to check your subtraction.

e.g. Is 125 − 89 = <u>36</u> correct?

```
  125
−  89
   36
```
→ If the sum of these 2 numbers is 125, '36' is the correct answer.

Check
```
   36
+  89
  125
```

125 − 89 = 36 is correct.

①
```
  573
− 209
  364  ◯
```
Check
```
  364
+ 209
```

②
```
  945
− 666
  289  ◯
```
Check
```
  +
```

③ 592 − 370 = __212__ ◯ Check 212   + 370   = _____

④ 827 − 489 = __338__ ◯ Check _____ + _____ = _____

⑤ 290 − 151 = __149__ ◯ Check _____ + _____ = _____

⑥ 600 − 512 = __88__ ◯ Check _____ + _____ = _____

⑦ 406 − 237 = __169__ ◯ Check _____ + _____ = _____

Solve the problems. Then check the answers.

⑧ Uncle Bill has picked 273 potatoes and Aunt Polly has picked 114 fewer. How many potatoes has Aunt Polly picked?

_____ potatoes

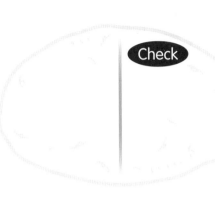

Check

⑨ There are 287 red onions and 148 white onions. How many more red onions than white onions are there?

_____ more

Check

⑩ Uncle Bill has picked 312 tomatoes. If he sells 219 tomatoes, how many tomatoes will be left?

_____ tomatoes

Check

⑪ What is the difference in the number of eggs collected in March and April?

Number of Eggs Collected	
March	531
April	680

Check

_____ eggs

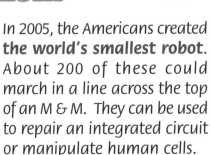

Did you know?

In 2005, the Americans created **the world's smallest robot.** About 200 of these could march in a line across the top of an M & M. They can be used to repair an integrated circuit or manipulate human cells.

DATE: _____

Day 20

Length and Distance (1)

Look at the picture. Choose the most appropriate unit to do each measurement. Write 'mm', 'cm', 'm', or 'km' in the circles.

①

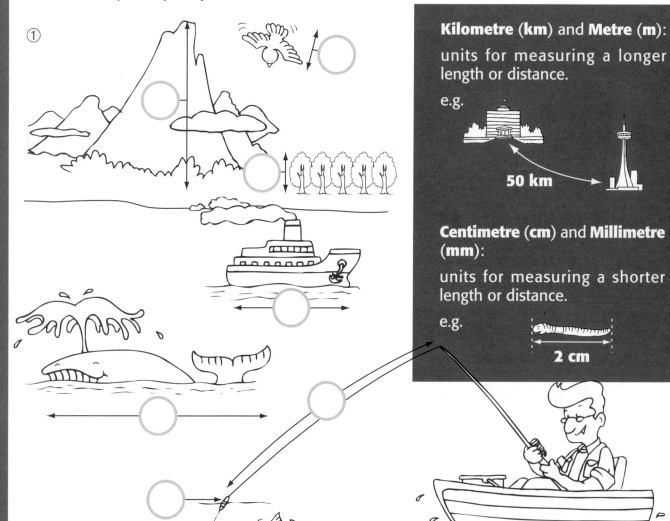

Kilometre (km) and **Metre (m)**:

units for measuring a longer length or distance.

e.g.

50 km

Centimetre (cm) and **Millimetre (mm)**:

units for measuring a shorter length or distance.

e.g.

2 cm

Draw lines to show the distances between the balls with the same pattern. Then measure each line and write your measurement in millimetres next to it.

②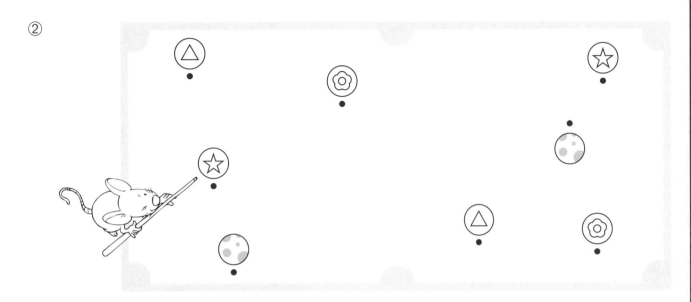

Look at the picture. Find the distances or lengths of the things. Then fill in the blanks with the given measurements.

15 m   350 m   8 m   3 km   3 m   85 m

③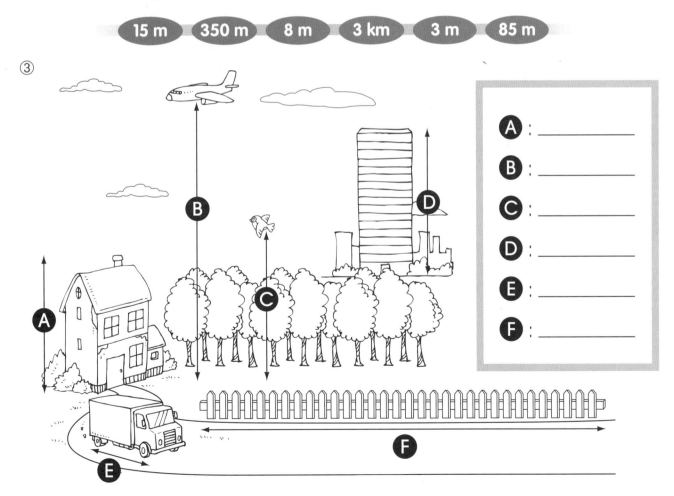

A : _____

B : _____

C : _____

D : _____

E : _____

F : _____

DATE: _____

Length and Distance (2)

Dinosaur Trail
1 km 20 m (1020 m)

You are here.

Fill in the blanks.

① 2 km = _____ m

② 30 mm = _____ cm

③ 6 cm = _____ mm

④ 4 m = _____ cm

⑤ 7 km = _____ m

⑥ 20 mm = _____ cm

⑦ 7 cm = _____ mm

⑧ 4000 m = _____ km

⑨ 3 km = _____ m

⑩ 5 km 600 m = _____ m

⑪ 2 cm 8 mm = _____ mm

⑫ 7 m 16 cm = _____ cm

> Remember the relationships between the units:
>
> 1 km = 1000 m
>
> 1 m = 100 cm
>
> 1 cm = 10 mm
>
> e.g. 2 km 3 m = 2000 m + 3 m
>   = 2003 m

Circle the best estimates.

⑬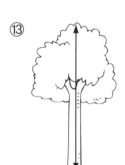

9 km

524 cm

96 mm

⑭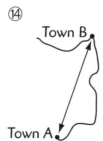

Town B

Town A

160 m

392 cm

15 km

⑮

22 cm

97 mm   30 m

Colour each container to show the amount of rainwater Eva collected last week. Then answer the questions.

⑯

Sun	5 mm
Mon	1 cm
Tue	16 mm
Wed	12 mm
Thu	8 mm
Fri	2 cm
Sat	15 mm

Sun   Mon   Tue   Wed   Thu   Fri   Sat

(rain gauge containers marked 20, 10, mm for each day)

⑰   What is the total amount of rain in mm collected
on Monday and Tuesday?   _____

⑱   What is the total amount of rain in cm collected
over the weekend?   _____

Look at the map. Solve the problems.

⑲   What is the total distance travelled
from D to A, and then to B?

_____ m

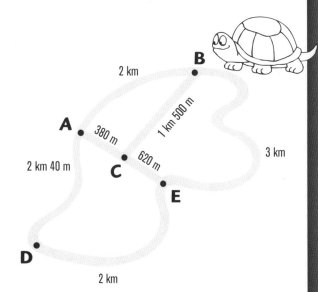

⑳   Find the shortest route from A to E.
Describe it. Then find the total
distance in km.

_____ ; _____

㉑   If a turtle can walk 500 m a day, how many days will it take to go
from B to C?

_____ days

Days and Years

I take about 365 days or 1 year to make one trip around the sun.

Sue is making a calendar for 2006. Help her make the pages for the missing months. Then circle the answer and fill in the blanks.

①

S	M	T	W	T	F	S

S	M	T	W	T	F	S

No. of Days		
	in Feb	in a Year
Normal Year	28	365
Leap Year	29	366

② 2006 is a leap / normal year.

③ Canada Day is on _____ , Halloween is on _____ , and Christmas Day is on _____ .

④ The first day of the year is _____ ; the last day is _____ .

Read what Andrew Alien says. Help him complete the calendar. Then answer the questions.

⑤

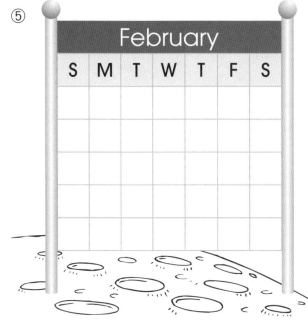

February						
S	M	T	W	T	F	S

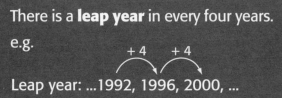

There is a **leap year** in every four years.

e.g.

$$\overset{+4}{\longrightarrow} \quad \overset{+4}{\longrightarrow}$$

Leap year: ...1992, 1996, 2000, ...

2008 is a leap year. The first day of February is a Friday.

⑥ There are _____ days in 2008.

⑦ The leap year right before 2008 is _____ .

⑧ The leap year right after 2008 is _____ .

⑨ Valentine's Day is on February _____ . It is on a _____ in 2008.

⑩ Andrew wants to send some Valentine cards to his friends on Earth. If it takes one month to deliver the cards, Andrew should send the cards on or before _____ .

⑪ If Andrew wants to visit his friends living on the Moon on the first day of each month, he will visit them _____ times a year.

⑫ *If I visit Toronto Zoo on the months that have 31 days, how many times will I visit the zoo in a year?*

_____ times

Did you know?

Except during World War I and II, **Olympic Summer Games** have been held every 4 years (in leap years) since 1896.

Day
23

Weeks and Years

This is my plan for you this year.

We have to do dishes for 52 weeks. We'll have no rest for almost a year.

Cats' Job: Week 1 – Week 52 Do Dishes

Look at the calendar. Fill in the blanks.

① Mr. Rice has a business trip in the second week of 2006. His trip is from _____ to _____ .

② If Mr. Rice takes a computer course which starts on Feb 15 and lasts for 3 weeks, he will finish the course on _____ .

③ Mr. Rice will start working on his proposal on the first day of February. If he completes his proposal on Mar 2, he will have taken about _____ weeks to do this project.

④

I would like to have my 2-week vacation in late March, but I have to be back on or before Apr 4. Can you suggest some suitable dates to start my vacation?

_____

2006

May						
S	M	T	W	T	F	S
	1	2	3	4	5	6
7	8	9	10	✗	12	13
14	15	16	17	18	19	20
21	22	23	24	25	26	27
28	29	30	31			

June						
S	M	T	W	T	F	S
				1	2	3
4	5	6	7	8	9	10
11	12	■	14	15	16	17
18	19	20	21	22	23	24
25	26	27	28	29	30	

July						
S	M	T	W	T	F	S
						1
2	3	4	5	6	7	8
9	10	11	12	13	14	15
16	17	18	19	20	21	22
■	24	25	26	27	28	29
30	31					

✗ – Disclosure of Experiment Results

■ – Conference

Look at Dr. Stein's schedule. Help him solve the problems.

⑤ Mother's Day is on the second Sunday of May. It is on May _____ .

⑥ Dr. Stein wants to disclose the success on his flower experiment to the public on _____ .

⑦ He has discovered a nutrient which can help flowers bloom for 9 weeks. If Dr. Stein gives his mother a flower with the nutrient on Mother's Day, the last day on which the flower still blooms will be _____ .

⑧ Father's Day is on the third Sunday of June. It is on June _____ .

⑨ Dr. Stein will attend a conference on _____ and _____ . The first conference is _____ days before Father's Day; the second one is _____ weeks after Father's Day.

Look at your own calendar. Then find how many weeks there are in the following periods.

⑩ From Jan 8 to Feb 12

_____ weeks

⑪ From Sep 14 to Oct 4

_____ weeks

⑫ From May 18 to Jun 14

_____ weeks

⑬ From Nov 28 to Dec 25

_____ weeks

DATE: _____

Telling Time

Draw the clock hands or
write the times on the
digital clocks. Then tell the times in words.

① `12:05`

_____

② `10:35`

_____

20 min
5 : 20

20 minutes past 5

50 min
6 : 50

10 minutes to 7

③

`[  :  ]`

_____

④

`[  :  ]`

_____

⑤

`[  :  ]`

_____

⑥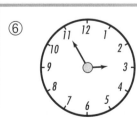

`[  :  ]`

_____

Show the times by using digital or analog clocks to complete the flyer. Then answer the questions.

Clown Show

⑦

Show A	Show B	Show C
May 13	May 14	May 15

Start

_____ : _____	_____ : _____	_____ : _____
20 min to 11	5 min past 3	10 min to 8

Finish

⑧ It takes Jimmy the clown 3 days to prepare for show A. When should Jimmy start to prepare?

_____

⑨ Jessica is going to watch show B. If she wants to arrive 5 minutes early, what time should she be there?

_____ : _____

⑩ If Cindy Clown wants to add a 10-minute break in Show C, what time will the show finish?

_____ : _____

Did you know?

Big Ben is the nickname of the Clock Tower in London, England. The tower is about 96 m tall with 4 clock faces.

Day
25

Passage of Time

You shouldn't toast me for more than 5 minutes!

Look at the baking guide on the oven. Draw clock hands or write numbers on the digital clocks to show what time the muffin or the pizza will be ready.

Bake for
30 min   28 min
On high

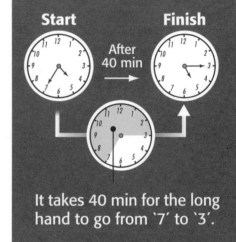

Start   Finish
After 40 min

It takes 40 min for the long hand to go from `7` to `3`.

①

If you start baking at	 will be ready at

②

If you start baking at	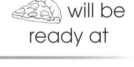 will be ready at
 05:25	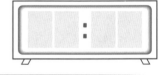
 07:53	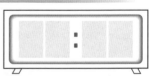

e.g. 03:29 → After 40 min → 04:09

```
  03:29
+    40
  04:09
```
Carry 60 min to the hour column.

Look at the arrival time of the train at each station. Find the time taken to travel between the stations. Then answer the questions.

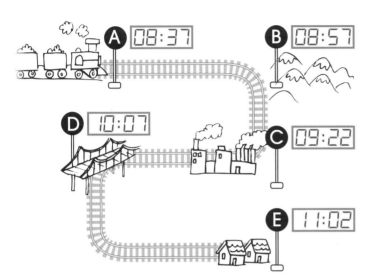

③

From	To	Time Taken
A	B	min
B	C	min
C	D	min
D	E	min

Sometimes you need to trade 1 h to 60 min to find the time interval.

e.g.   From 3:45 to 4:05

$$\begin{array}{r} 4:05 \\ -\ 3:45 \end{array} \xrightarrow[\text{to 60 min}]{\text{trade 1 h}} \begin{array}{r} \overset{3\quad 65}{4:05} \\ -\ 3:45 \\ \hline 20 \end{array}$$

The time interval is 20 min.

④   How long is the trip from A to C?

_____ min

⑤   If Joe catches the next train at Station A at 10:23, what time will he reach Station C?

_____

Fill in the blanks.

⑥   Sean starts watching a TV show at 5:05. If the show lasts 42 minutes, it will end at _____ .

⑦   Joan let her cat out at 10 minutes to 2. The cat came home at 2:30; it had stayed outside for _____ min.

⑧   Reading a book:

Start    Finish

Time taken: ____ h ____ min

Did you know?

The **Express train** takes about 4 hours and 15 minutes to travel from Toronto to Montreal.

Temperatures

I like summer and winter!

Dr. Stein has done experiments on four different substances. Help him record the temperatures of the substances after the experiments. Then read the clues to label the test tubes with the names of the substances and answer the questions.

①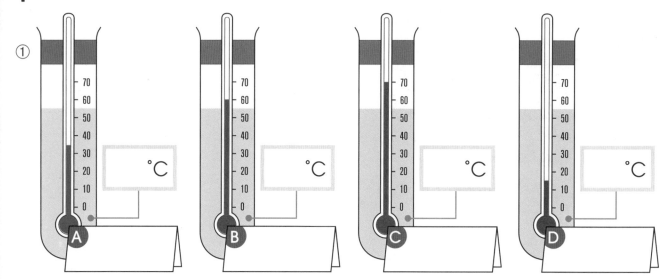

Results of the experiments:

• The temperature of 'Sydex' is higher than that of 'Combex'.
• The temperature of 'Raium' is 25°C lower than that of 'Combex'.
• 'Katium' has the lowest temperature.

② Which substance has the highest temperature? _____

③ If the temperature of 'Raium' drops 5°C every hour, what will be its temperature after 2 hours? _____

What are the temperatures of the liquids? Match the pictures with the correct measurements. Then answer the questions.

④

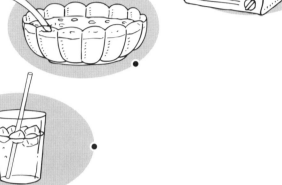

- 2°C

- 10°C

- 15°C

- 70°C

- 98°C

⑤ If Judy pours the water in **C** into **B**, the temperature of the liquid in **B** will   decrease / increase . The temperature might become   2°C / 8°C / 12°C .

⑥ If Katie pours the water in **D** and the tea in **E** into a bowl, the temperature of the mixture   will / will not   be higher than 70°C. The temperature might become   52°C / 92°C / 12°C .

⑦ If Ted puts **C** outside, the ice disappears in a short time. What do you think the season is?

_____

Perimeter

The perimeter of our model farm is 140 cm.

20 cm

50 cm

Find the perimeter of each shape.

Perimeter is the distance around the outside of a shape.

e.g.

1 cm

2 cm   2 cm

1 cm

Perimeter:
1 + 2 + 1 + 2
= 6 (cm)

All the sides of a regular shape are the same in length.

①

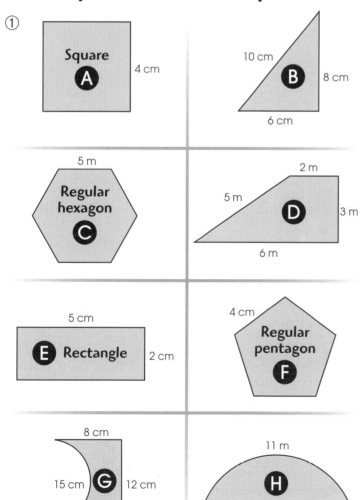

Square
A
4 cm

10 cm
B
8 cm
6 cm

5 m
Regular hexagon
C

2 m
5 m
D
3 m
6 m

5 cm
E Rectangle
2 cm

4 cm
Regular pentagon
F

8 cm
15 cm **G** 12 cm
8 cm

11 m
H
7 m

A _____

B _____

C _____

D _____

E _____

F _____

G _____

H _____

Draw 2 different rectangles that both have a perimeter of 20 cm.

②

Solve the problems.

③ Jason has used a wire to form a rectangle. If he bends the wire into a triangle, how long is the third side?

Perimeter of the rectangle: ____ + ____ + ____ + ____ = ____ (cm)

Length of the third side: ____ − ____ − ____ = ____ (cm)

④ If Louis cuts the rectangle along the dotted lines to make four identical rectangles, what is the perimeter of each small rectangle?

Length of the small rectangle:

_____ = ____ (cm)

Perimeter of the small rectangle:

_____

= ____ (cm)

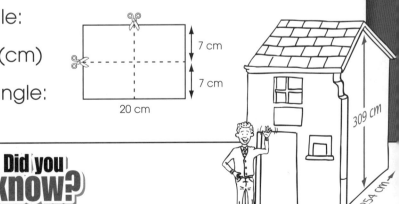

For question ④, use division to find the length of the small rectangle.

Did you know?

The **smallest house** in the world is located in Conwy, Wales, U.K.

Area

The area covered by the tent is about the same as the total area of 3 sleeping bags.

Count and write the number of squares needed to cover the stickers. Then answer the questions.

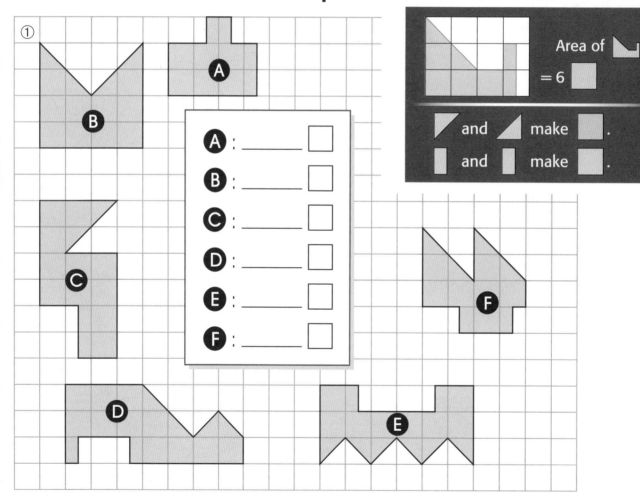

①

A : _____ ▢

B : _____ ▢

C : _____ ▢

D : _____ ▢

E : _____ ▢

F : _____ ▢

Area of ⌐_∖ = 6 ▢

◸ and ◺ make ▢.

▯ and ▯ make ▢.

② Which shape has the greatest area? _____

③ Which shape has the smallest area? _____

Draw lines to make a grid. Then use coloured pencils to help the children draw their shapes and label the shapes with their names.

④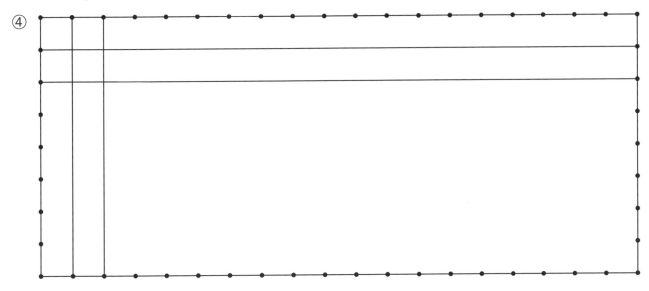

⑤

My rectangle has an area of 8 square units. I call it 'Rectango'.

Lisa

⑥

I like squares. I have a square with an area of 9 small square units. I call it 'Mr. Square'.

Gary

⑦

My favorite shape is the triangle. My triangle has an area of 8 square units. I call it 'Triango'.

Amanda

Look at the children's shapes again. Answer the questions.

⑧ If Amanda uses two 'Triangos' to form a 4-sided shape, what shape will she get? Will the shape have an area that is greater than that of 'Mr. Square'?

_____ ; _____

⑨ If Lisa cuts her 'Rectango' into two identical triangles, what is the area of each triangle?

_____ square units

Day
29

Money (1)

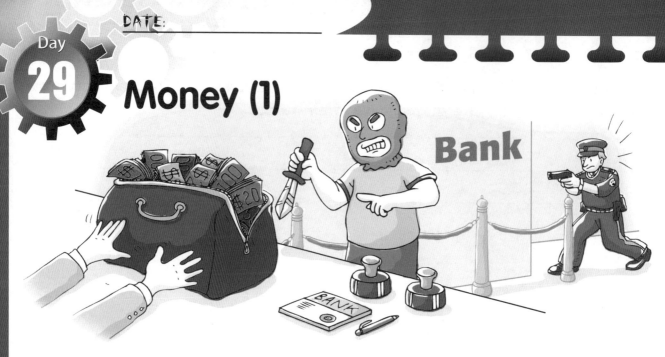

Match the bills with their values.

- $5 -
- $10 -
- $20 -
- $50 -
- $100 -

Check ✔ the correct number of bills to trade the bill in the circle.

②

③

Find the amount that each person has. Then solve the problems.

④

Mr. Wolf

Aunt Isabel

Uncle Peter

_____   _____   _____

⑤ Who has the most money?   _____

⑥ Who has the least money?   _____

⑦ How much more does Aunt Isabel have than
Uncle Peter?   _____ more

Find the amount in each group.

⑧

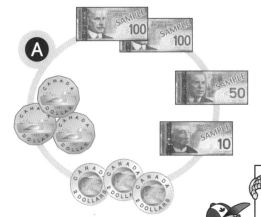

A

B

A : _____

B : _____

Did you know?

The world's **largest bank robbery** occurred in 1945. About $580 million (US) were taken from Reichsbank in Berlin, Germany.

DATE: _____

Money (2)

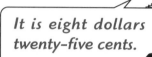

$ 8.25

Is it eight hundred twenty-five dollars? ✗

It is eight dollars twenty-five cents. ✓

Find the amount in each group and write it in 2 different ways.

①

There are two ways to write money amounts.

e.g.

Amount: **2 dollars 26 cents**
$2.26

Amount

 _____ ; $ _____

 _____ ; $ _____

 _____ ; $ _____

 _____ ; $ _____

 _____ ; $ _____

Use the fewest coins and bills to show the amounts.

 = **$100**

 = **$50**

 = **$20**

 = **$10**

 = **$5**

 = **$2**

 = **$1**

 = **25¢**

 = **10¢**

 = **5¢**

 = **1¢**

② $52.26

$50 _____

③ 85 dollars 65 cents

_____

④ $34.77

_____

⑤ 102 dollars 32 cents

_____

⑥ $63.23

_____

⑦ 37 dollars 5 cents

_____

Suggest 2 ways to solve the riddle by drawing coins and bills.

⑧

> I have $30.41. There are 3 bills and 5 coins in all.

1st way

2nd way

DATE: _____

Addition and Subtraction with Money

Money Saved

Dollar	Cent
4	115
5̸	1̸5
− 3	28
1	87

Total

Dollar	Cent
2	39
+ 2	15
4	54

$2.15

$2.39

Special

$3.28
Reg. $5.15

Find the total cost and price difference of each pair of toys.

①  $5.55 $4.19

Dollar	Cent		Dollar	Cent

+ _____   − _____
    TOTAL   DIFFERENCE

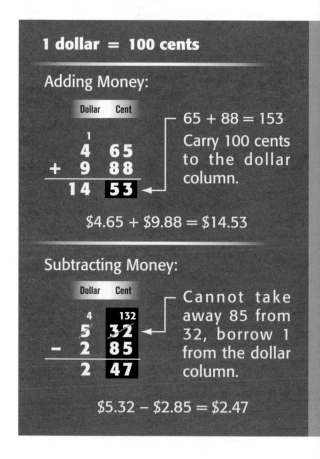

1 dollar = 100 cents

Adding Money:

Dollar	Cent
¹	
4	65
+ 9	88
14	53

65 + 88 = 153
Carry 100 cents to the dollar column.

$4.65 + $9.88 = $14.53

Subtracting Money:

Dollar	Cent
4	132
5̸	3̸2̸
− 2	85
2	47

Cannot take away 85 from 32, borrow 1 from the dollar column.

$5.32 − $2.85 = $2.47

---

②  $6.43 $2.88

Dollar	Cent		Dollar	Cent

+ _____   − _____
    TOTAL   DIFFERENCE

Find the answers.

③ $5.39 + $3.77 = _____   ④ $9.24 − $4.83 = _____

⑤ $7.29 − $1.54 = _____   ⑥ $3.65 + $2.17 = _____

Solve the problems.

⑦ Emma has $7.59 and Jimmy has $2.18.

    a. How much do the children have in all?

        Dollar   Cent

        $ _____ in all

    b. How much more does Emma have than Jimmy?

        Dollar   Cent

        $ _____ more

⑧ A bottle of juice costs $5.29.

    a. How much do two bottles of juice cost in all?

        Dollar   Cent

        $ _____ in all

    b. If a bottle of juice costs 45¢ less now, what is its price?

        Dollar   Cent

        $ _____

⑨ A bag of chips costs $2.75.

    a. A lollipop costs 18¢ less than a bag of chips. How much does a lollipop cost?

        Dollar   Cent

        $ _____

    b. If Zoey buys a bag of chips and a lollipop, how much does she need to pay in all?

        Dollar   Cent

        $ _____ in all

    c. How much do two bags of chips cost in all?

        Dollar   Cent

        $ _____ in all

Did you know?

The world's largest **popsicle** was made in Hellendoom, the Netherlands in 1997. It weighed about 9075 kg!

Capacity (1)

It can drink 10 L of pop at a time.

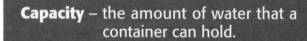

Circle the reasonable capacities.

> **Capacity** – the amount of water that a container can hold.
>
> ___
>
> **Litre** is a big unit for measuring capacity. e.g.
>
> The capacity of this pot is about 5 L.

①

10 L
3 L
300 L

②

4 L
10 L
100 L

③

250 L
1 L
50 L

④

40 L
125 L
2 L

⑤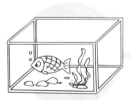

25 L
2 L
188 L

⑥

1 L
15 L
40 L

⑦

5 L
480 L
75 L

Label the containers with the given capacities.

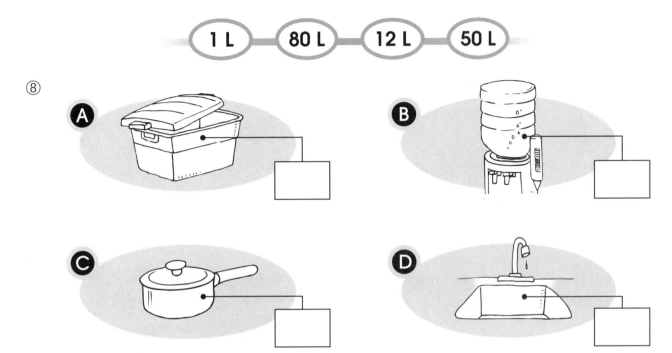

(1 L)—(80 L)—(12 L)—(50 L)

⑧

A ☐

B ☐

C ☐

D ☐

Solve the problems.

⑨ If Mr. Brown uses a tin of paint to paint his bedroom with 4 walls about the same size, about how much paint is used on each wall?

_____

⑩ Mrs. Brown makes about 1 L of orange juice with 12 oranges. If she wants to make 3 L of orange juice, how many oranges does she need?

_____

⑪ Which hold more, 2 buckets or 3 jugs?

_____

⑫ How much gasoline do 4 cars hold?

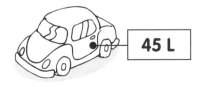

45 L

_____

Day
33

Capacity (2)

Record the capacity of each container.
Then answer the questions.

①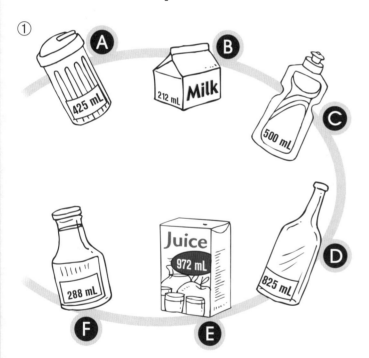

Millilitre is a small unit for measuring capacity.

e.g.

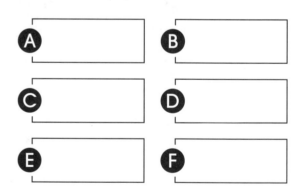

The capacity of a teaspoon is about 5 mL.

1 L	**=**	**1000 mL**
Half a Litre	**=**	**500 mL**

Ⓐ [   ] Ⓑ [   ]

Ⓒ [   ] Ⓓ [   ]

Ⓔ [   ] Ⓕ [   ]

② Which container has the greatest capacity? _____

③ Which container has the least capacity? _____

④ Which containers have a capacity less than half a litre? _____

⑤ How many millilitres of water can 2 Ⓐ hold? _____

⑥ How much greater is the capacity of 1 Ⓔ than 1 Ⓑ ? _____

⑦ Which 2 containers together have the same capacity as 1 Ⓒ ? _____

Find and record the capacity of each container.

5 mL   30 mL   250 mL

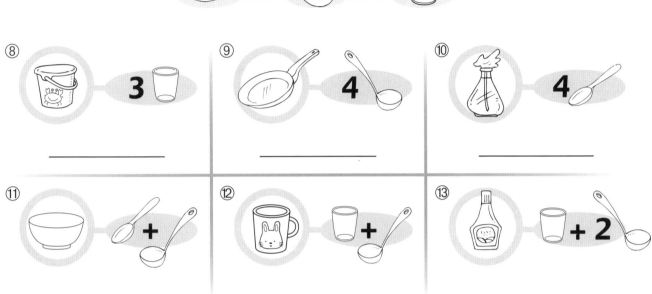

⑧ [bucket] — **3** [cup]

_____

⑨ [pan] — **4** [ladle]

_____

⑩ [bag] — **4** [spoon]

_____

⑪ [bowl] — [spoon] **+** [ladle]

_____

⑫ [mug] — [cup] **+** [spoon]

_____

⑬ [bottle] — [cup] **+ 2** [ladle]

_____

The children are making fruit punch. Help them draw lines to find the best bowls to hold the drinks.

⑭

Fruit Punch

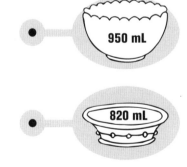

a. 250 mL   258 mL   355 mL   •   • 950 mL

b. 325 mL   245 mL   375 mL   •   • 820 mL

c. 400 mL   189 mL   200 mL   •   • 880 mL

d. 150 mL   500 mL   320 mL   •   • 1 L

DATE: _____

Mass (1)

30 kg?

Circle the best estimate of the mass of each object.

①

2 kg
5 kg
10 kg

②

5 kg
1 kg
10 kg

③

40 kg
2 kg
8 kg

④

3 kg
500 kg
80 kg

The **kilogram (kg)** is a big unit for measuring mass.

e.g.

55 kg

Record the mass of each item.

⑤ 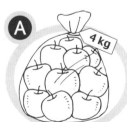 A — 4 kg

 B — 5 kg

 C — Potatoes 10 kg

 D — coffee 2 kg

 E — Lollipops 3 kg

 F — Sausage 1 kg

A _____

B _____

C _____

D _____

E _____

F _____

Record the weight of each person. Then answer the questions.

⑥

Eva	Weight
2 Years ago	28 kg
Now	

⑦

Martin	Weight
2 Years ago	22 kg
Now	

⑧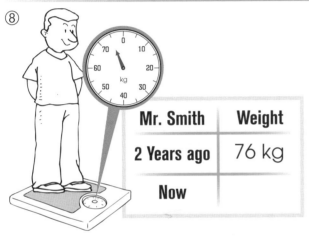

Mr. Smith	Weight
2 Years ago	76 kg
Now	

⑨

Mrs. Smith	Weight
2 Years ago	59 kg
Now	

⑩ Eva was _____ kg heavier than Martin two years ago.

⑪ Martin is _____ kg lighter than Eva now.

⑫ Mrs. Smith was _____ kg lighter than Mr. Smith two years ago.

⑬ Mr. Smith is _____ kg heavier than Mrs. Smith now.

⑭ Did each person gain or lose weight in the past two years? Circle the correct word and fill in the blank.

Eva: gain / lose ; _____ kg

Martin: gain / lose ; _____ kg

Mr. Smith: gain / lose ; _____ kg

Mrs. Smith: gain / lose ; _____ kg

Did you know?

The heaviest cat on record was Himmy, who lived in Queensland, Australia. He weighed about 21 kg in 1986.

REVIEW

Fill in the missing information to complete the table. Then answer the questions.

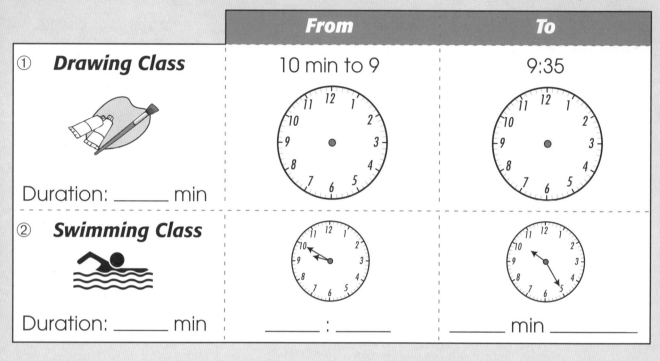

	From	**To**
① **Drawing Class** Duration: _____ min	10 min to 9	9:35
② **Swimming Class** Duration: _____ min	_____ : _____	_____ min _____

③ If Erica attends the drawing class and swimming class every Saturday, how long is her break? _____

④ If the classes start on Feb 3, Erica will have her next classes on Feb _____ .

Find the amount in each group and write in 2 different ways. Then find the total amount and the difference.

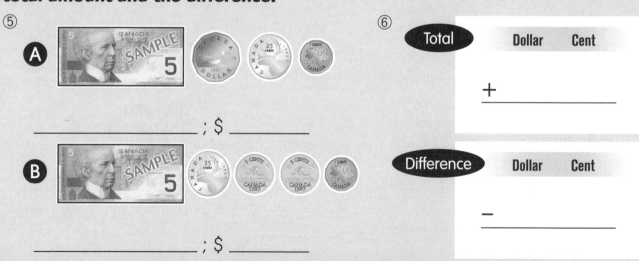

⑤

Ⓐ _____ ; $ _____

Ⓑ _____ ; $ _____

⑥

Total	Dollar	Cent
	+ _____	

Difference	Dollar	Cent
	− _____	

Check the answers by using addition. Put a check mark ✔ in the circle if the answer is correct; otherwise, put a cross ✗.

⑦   427 – 189   = <u> 238 </u> ◯

⑧   605 – 416   = <u> 189 </u> ◯

⑨   310 – 128   = <u> 173 </u> ◯

⑩   532 – 216   = <u> 306 </u> ◯

Check

Find the answers.

⑪ $3.29 + $1.85   = _____

⑫ $2.57 + $4.68   = _____

⑬ $4.81 – $0.63   = _____

⑭ $5.94 – $3.28   = _____

⑮ $7.19 – $6.84   = _____

⑯ $3.76 + $3.76   = _____

Find the perimeter and area of each shape.

⑰

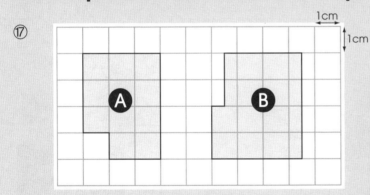

1cm
1cm

	Perimeter	Area
A	cm	cm²
B	cm	cm²

Record the measurements.

⑱

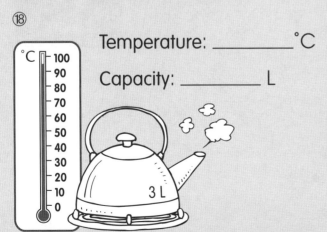

Temperature: _____ °C

Capacity: _____ L

⑲

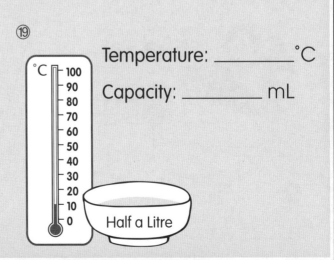

Temperature: _____ °C

Capacity: _____ mL

DATE: _____

You Deserve A Break!

A $5.29

B Cookies $2.49

C $4.35

D Potato Chips $3.50

Put the items in order. Start with the most expensive one. Write the letters in the circles and the costs of the items on the lines.

① ◯ : _____ dollars _____ cents

◯ : _____ dollars _____ cents

◯ : _____ dollars _____ cents

◯ : _____ dollars _____ cents

Find the lengths of the things. Fill in the blanks with the given measurements.

②

③

Length in Total

40 Rolls

④

⑤

⑥

40 mm
1 km
68 cm
5 m
24 cm

Record the capacities of the containers. Then match them with the correct descriptions.

⑦ _____ •

_____ •

_____ •

_____ •

• has the greatest capacity

• holds 2 times a litre

• has the smallest capacity

• holds almost a litre

2 L

4 L

POP 385 mL

982 mL

Use the calendar to complete the poster.

The leap year right after 2004

NOV

S	M	T	W	T	F	S
						1
2	3	4	5	6	7	8
9	10	11	12	13	14	15
The current 2-week special						29
30						

2-Week *Special*

⑧ From
Nov _____ , 20 _____
to
Nov _____ , 20 _____

Next 2-Week *Special*

⑨ From
_____
to
_____

There is a promotion every 2 weeks.

DATE:

Mass (2)

Cake

Flour	150 g
Sugar	20 g
Butter	5 g
Salt	2 g

Draw a line to match each object with the best estimate of its mass.

①

950 g   100 g   250 g   15 g   50 g

The **gram (g)** is a small unit for measuring mass.

e.g.

 A can of tuna weighs about 120 g.

 A bag of chips weighs about 80 g.

Record the mass of each object.

②
140 g

③
Chocolate **420 g**

④
Cereal **950 g**

⑤
Cup Noodles **85 g**

⑥
Sunflower Seeds **820 g**

⑦
Chicken **90 g**

⑧
Marshmallows **125 g**

⑨
Crackers **275 g**

Find and record the mass of each item. Then answer the questions.

⑩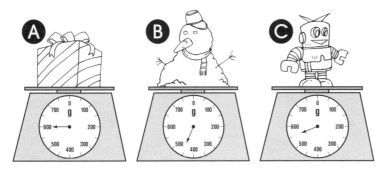

A _____

B _____

C _____

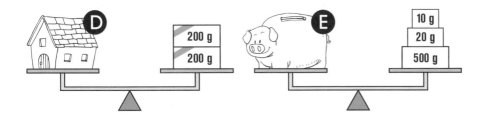

D _____

E _____

⑪ Which items are heavier than 500 g? _____

⑫ Which items are heavier than the snowman? _____

⑬ How many | 200 g | are needed to balance the
weight of the gift box? _____

Use the given weights to balance each item.

| 200 g | 100 g | 50 g | 10 g |

Use the fewest weights to balance each one.

⑭

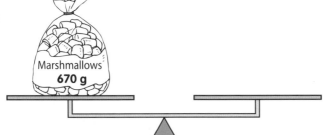

Cookies

560 g

⑮

Marshmallows
670 g

Did you know?

A serving (28 g) of **chocolate cake** prepared with chocolate frosting contains about 5 g of fat.

Multiplying by 2, 5, or 0

$$\begin{array}{r} 5 \\ \times\ 3 \\ \hline 1\ 5 \end{array}$$

DATE: _____

There are 3 groups of 5 stars – 15 stars in all.

Do the multiplication with the help of each group of pictures.

①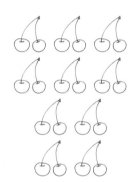

   a.   3 x 2 = _____   b.   8 x 2 = _____

   c.   5 x 2 = _____   d.   6 x 2 = _____

   e.   2 x 2 = _____   f.   1 x 2 = _____

   g.   9 x 2 = _____   h.   4 x 2 = _____

   i.   7 x 2 = _____   j.   10 x 2 = _____

②

   a.   5 x 0 = _____   b.   3 x 0 = _____

   c.   2 x 0 = _____   d.   4 x 0 = _____

   e.   6 x 0 = _____   f.   1 x 0 = _____

③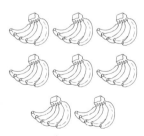

   a.   5 x 5 = _____   b.   7 x 5 = _____

   c.   4 x 5 = _____   d.   2 x 5 = _____

   e.   1 x 5 = _____   f.   3 x 5 = _____

   g.   9 x 5 = _____   h.   8 x 5 = _____

   i.   6 x 5 = _____   j.   10 x 5 = _____

Use the pictures to solve the problems.

④ How many lollipops are there in 6 boxes of lollipops?

_____ x _____ = _____   _____ lollipops

⑤ How many lollipops are there in 9 boxes of lollipops?

_____ x _____ = _____   _____ lollipops

⑥ Each girl has a pair of hairclips. How many hairclips do 8 girls have in all?

_____ x _____ = _____   _____ hairclips

⑦ How many eyes do 7 aliens have in all?

_____ x _____ = _____   _____ eyes

⑧ How many hands do 5 aliens have in all?

_____ x _____ = _____   _____ hands

⑨ There is no fish in the fish bowl.

　a. How many fish are there in 3 fish bowls?

　　_____ x _____ = _____

　　_____ fish

　b. How many fish are there in 9 fish bowls?

　　_____ x _____

　　= _____

　　_____ fish

Did you know?

Stars are classified according to their size and brightness. Our Sun is a G2, which is very close to the middle of the range.

Day
39

Multiplying by 1, 3, or 4

There are 2 groups of 3 pigs – 6 pigs in all.

$$\begin{array}{r} 3 \\ \times\ 2 \\ \hline 6 \end{array}$$

Do the multiplication with the help of each group of pictures.

①

a.
$$\begin{array}{r} 3 \\ \times\ 8 \\ \hline \end{array}$$

b.
$$\begin{array}{r} 3 \\ \times\ 6 \\ \hline \end{array}$$

c.   4 x 3 = _____

d.   5 x 3 = _____

e.   2 x 3 = _____

f.   7 x 3 = _____

g.   9 x 3 = _____

②

a.
$$\begin{array}{r} 1 \\ \times\ 9 \\ \hline \end{array}$$

b.
$$\begin{array}{r} 1 \\ \times\ 7 \\ \hline \end{array}$$

c.   6 x 1 = _____

d.   5 x 1 = _____

e.   2 x 1 = _____

f.   8 x 1 = _____

g.   3 x 1 = _____

③

a.
$$\begin{array}{r} 4 \\ \times\ 9 \\ \hline \end{array}$$

b.
$$\begin{array}{r} 4 \\ \times\ 5 \\ \hline \end{array}$$

c.   3 x 4 = _____

d.   6 x 4 = _____

e.   7 x 4 = _____

f.   2 x 4 = _____

g.   1 x 4 = _____

Solve the problems.

④ There are 3 potatoes in a basket. How many potatoes in all are there in 7 baskets?

_____ potatoes

⑤ Uncle Tim puts 4 eggplants in a bag. How many eggplants are there in 6 bags?

_____ eggplants

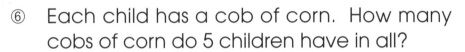

⑥ Each child has a cob of corn. How many cobs of corn do 5 children have in all?

_____ cobs of corn

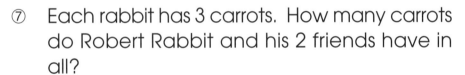

⑦ Each rabbit has 3 carrots. How many carrots do Robert Rabbit and his 2 friends have in all?

_____ carrots

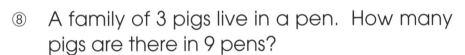

⑧ A family of 3 pigs live in a pen. How many pigs are there in 9 pens?

_____ pigs

Day
40

Multiplying by 6 or 7

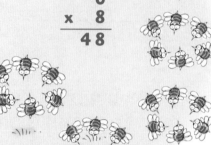

There are 6 bees in a group.

There are 48 bees.

Circle the animals. Then do the multiplications.

① Circle every 6 ants.

a. 5 x 6 = _____   b. 3 x 6 = _____   c. 7 x 6 = _____

d. 1 x 6 = _____   e. 9 x 6 = _____   f. 4 x 6 = _____

g. 2 x 6 = _____   h. 6 x 6 = _____   i. 10 x 6 = _____

② Circle every 7 dragonflies.

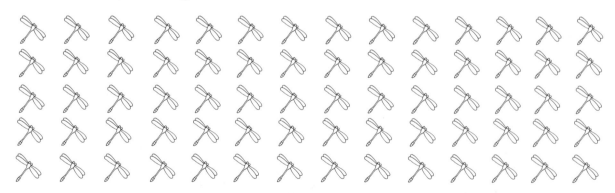

a. 2 x 7 = _____   b. 6 x 7 = _____   c. 4 x 7 = _____

d. 3 x 7 = _____   e. 9 x 7 = _____   f. 1 x 7 = _____

g. 5 x 7 = _____   h. 8 x 7 = _____   i. 7 x 7 = _____

Look at the pictures. Solve the problems.

③ How many muffins are there in 5 boxes?

_____ = _____

_____ muffins

④ How many apples are there in 3 baskets?

_____ = _____

_____ apples

⑤ How many children are there in 4 groups?

_____ = _____

_____ children

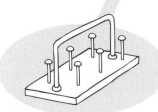

⑥ How many cups can 9 cup holders hold?

_____ = _____

_____ cups

⑦ *How many storybooks are there in 3 sets?*

_____ = _____

_____ storybooks

⑧ *How much do 5 sets cost?*

$7

_____

= _____

$ _____

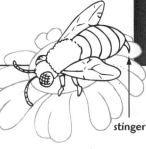

Did you know?

stinger

Worker bees are infertile females. Each worker bee has a stinger with which she can sting to defend the hive, but she will die soon after.

Multiplying by 8 or 9

Each necklace has 8 beads.

There are 40 beads in all.

```
  8
x 5
———
 40
```

Find the answers.

①
```
  8
x 3
———
```

②
```
  9
x 2
———
```

③
```
  9
x 5
———
```

④
```
  8
x 2
———
```

⑤ 7 x 8 = _____

⑥ 3 x 9 = _____

⑦ 9 x 9 = _____

⑧ 6 x 9 = _____

⑨ 4 x 8 = _____

⑩ 9 x 8 = _____

⑪ 4 x 9 = _____

⑫ 6 x 8 = _____

⑬ 10 x 9 = _____

Follow the order of the answers to help Billy Bird find his way home.

⑭

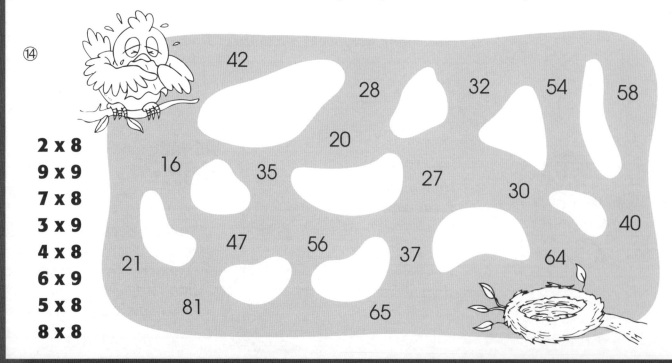

2 x 8
9 x 9
7 x 8
3 x 9
4 x 8
6 x 9
5 x 8
8 x 8

42   28   32   54   58

20

16   35   27   30

47   56   37   40

21   64

81   65

Look at the pictures. Complete the tables and answer the questions.

⑮

No. of Boxes	4	5	6	7
No. of Chocolates in all				
Cost ($)				

⑯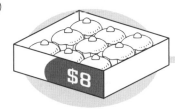

No. of Boxes	3	6	8	9
No. of Muffins in all				
Cost ($)				

⑰ Mr. Welch buys 3 boxes of chocolates.
   How much does he need to pay?

   _____ = _____ $ _____

⑱ Jack buys 2 boxes of muffins. How
   many muffins does he buy in all?

   _____ = _____   _____ muffins

⑲ How many chocolates are there in 8
   boxes?

   _____ = _____   _____ chocolates

Question ⑳ is a 2-step problem. Find how much Amy needs to pay for each goup of items first. Then use addition to find the amount.

⑳

If I buy 2 boxes of chocolates and 1 box of muffins, how much do I need to pay?

Amy

_____ = _____

_____ = _____

$ _____

Did you know?

Beads were made from the seeds of the Bead Tree before being replaced by plastics and other materials.

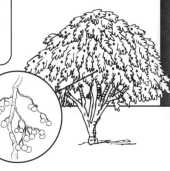

Solving Problems Involving Multiplication

No. of ● :
```
    5
x   3
-----
   15
```

No. of ★ :
```
    4
x   5
-----
   20
```

Tina has drawn 3 rows of 5 circles and 5 rows of 4 stars.

Use the pictures to solve the problems.

①  How many balloons are there

    a. in 6 bags?   _____ balloons

    b. in 9 bags?   _____ balloons

②  How many pieces of chicken breast are there

    a. in 3 packs?   _____ pieces

    b. in 8 packs?   _____ pieces

③  How many crayons are there

    a. in 2 boxes?   _____ crayons

    b. in 7 boxes?   _____ crayons

④  How many batteries are there

    a. in 1 pack?   _____ batteries

    b. in 5 packs?   _____ batteries

DATE: _____

Solve the problems.

⑤ There are 9 apples in a bag. If Mr. White buys 4 bags of apples, how many apples will he buy in all?

_____ apples

⑥ There are 3 candies in a box. If Judy and her 2 sisters have a box of candies each, how many candies do the girls have in all?

_____ candies

⑦ A roll of ribbon can make 4 flowers. If Annie has 7 rolls of ribbon, how many flowers willl she make?

_____ flowers

⑧ Each toy car costs 8¢. How much in total do 9 toy cars cost?

_____ ¢

⑨ Ken used some triangles to make a tree. How many triangles does he need to make 5 trees?

_____ triangles

DATE: _____

More about Multiplication

There are 5 columns of 3 flowers.

There are 3 rows of 5 flowers.

$3 \times 5 = 5 \times 3 = 15$

Each pair of pictures have the same number of fruits. Draw the correct number of fruit so that each container has the same amount. Then fill in the blanks.

①

5×4 = $4 \times \underline{\hspace{1cm}}$

②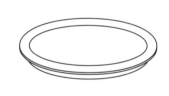

3×2 = $2 \times \underline{\hspace{1cm}}$

③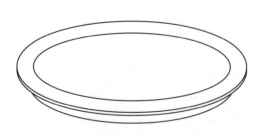

4×1 = $1 \times \underline{\hspace{1cm}}$

Find the answers. Then circle the correct word to complete what Christie says.

④   3 x 8   = _____   ⑤   6 x 7   = _____   ⑥   5 x 4   = _____

      8 x 3   = _____   7 x 6   = _____   4 x 5   = _____

⑦   2 x 9   = _____   ⑧   3 x 6   = _____   ⑨   7 x 8   = _____

      9 x 2   = _____   6 x 3   = _____   8 x 7   = _____

⑩   7 x 9   = _____   ⑪   5 x 8   = _____   ⑫   2 x 6   = _____

      9 x 7   = _____   8 x 5   = _____   6 x 2   = _____

⑬   Though the order of multiplication has changed, the difference / sum / product is still the same.

$$3 \times 5 = 5 \times 3$$

Each set of twins has the same number of beads or marbles. Read what they say. Then answer the question.

⑭

Sonia   Sally

My sister has 6 necklaces with 5 beads in each. I have 5 necklaces. How many beads are there in each of my necklaces?

_____ beads

⑮   *My brother has 9 boxes of 4 marbles. I have 4 boxes. How many marbles are there in each of my boxes?*

Ted   Tim   _____ marbles

Did you know?

Only 4 out of the 20 000 known species of bees are considered **honeybees**. They probably originated in Africa since the time of the building of the Egyptian pyramids.

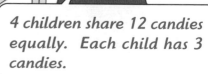

Day 44

Introducing Division

4 children share 12 candies equally. Each child has 3 candies.

DATE: _____

Draw the pictures. Then help the children solve the problems.

①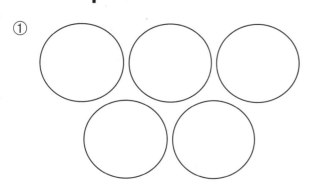

a. Draw 3 marbles in each circle.

There are _____ marbles in all.

b. If Joey puts 15 marbles equally into 5 groups, there will be _____ marbles in each group.

②

a. Draw 4 leaves in each box.

There are _____ leaves in all.

b. If Tina puts 24 leaves equally into 6 groups, there will be _____ leaves in each group.

③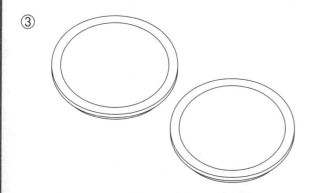

a. Draw 2 spoons on each plate.

There are _____ spoons in all.

b. If Mrs. Stein puts 4 spoons equally into 2 groups, there will be _____ spoons in each group.

Circle the toys into groups. Then fill in the blanks.

④

There are 4 tops in each group.

Jessica has _____ tops. If she puts every 4 tops into a group, she will have _____ groups of tops.

⑤

There are 2 cars in each group.

Donald has _____ cars. If he puts every 2 cars into a group, he will have _____ groups of cars.

⑥

There are 5 blocks in each group.

Anita has _____ blocks. If she puts every 5 blocks into a group, she will have _____ groups of blocks.

⑦

There are 3 rockets in each group.

Ray has _____ rockets. If he puts every 3 rockets into a group, he will have _____ groups of rockets.

DATE: _____

Day 45 Dividing by 1, 2, or 3

I can have 6 carrots.

Each of us can have 3 carrots.

Each of us can have 2 carrots.

Use the pictures to find the answers. Then do the long division.

①  $2\overline{)8}$

$8 \div 2 =$ _____

② 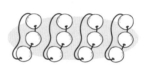 $3\overline{)12}$

$12 \div 3 =$ _____

③  $1\overline{)5}$

$5 \div 1 =$ _____

④  $2\overline{)10}$

$10 \div 2 =$ _____

Do the division with the help of the pictures.

⑤

a. $18 \div 2 =$ _____   b. $6 \div 2 =$ _____

c. $14 \div 2 =$ _____   d. $12 \div 2 =$ _____

⑥

a. $18 \div 3 =$ _____   b. $9 \div 3 =$ _____

c. $21 \div 3 =$ _____   d. $15 \div 3 =$ _____

Find the answers.

⑦

$3\overline{)12}$

⑧

$2\overline{)14}$

⑨

$3\overline{)24}$

⑩

$1\overline{)8}$

⑪ 10 ÷ 2 = _____

⑫ 15 ÷ 3 = _____

⑬ 9 ÷ 1 = _____

⑭ 27 ÷ 3 = _____

⑮ 4 ÷ 2 = _____

⑯ 18 ÷ 2 = _____

⑰ 6 ÷ 1 = _____

⑱ 7 ÷ 1 = _____

⑲ 9 ÷ 3 = _____

Use the pictures to solve the problems.

⑳

Annie has a box of cookies. If she shares the cookies with 2 of her friends, how many cookies will each child get?

_____ = _____   _____ cookies

㉑ If Uncle Billy divides a box of soup into 2 groups, how many cans of soup will there be in each group?

_____ = _____   _____ cans of soup

㉒

Jimmy and Lucy share a pack of candies. How many candies does each child get?

_____

= _____

_____ candies

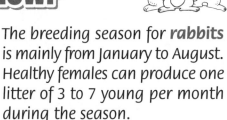

Did you know?

The breeding season for **rabbits** is mainly from January to August. Healthy females can produce one litter of 3 to 7 young per month during the season.

Day 46

Dividing by 4 or 5

5 seals share 15 rings.

$15 \div 5 = 3$

Find the answers with the help of the pictures.

①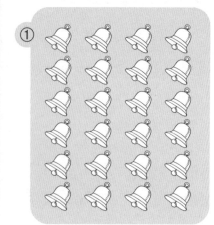

a. $4\overline{)24}$

b. $4\overline{)16}$

c. $20 \div 4 =$ _____

d. $8 \div 4 =$ _____

e. $4 \div 4 =$ _____

f. $12 \div 4 =$ _____

②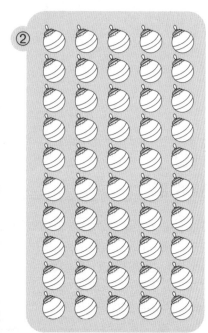

a. $5\overline{)35}$

b. $5\overline{)25}$

c. $20 \div 5 =$ _____

d. $40 \div 5 =$ _____

e. $15 \div 5 =$ _____

f. $5 \div 5 =$ _____

g. $10 \div 5 =$ _____

h. $45 \div 5 =$ _____

i. $30 \div 5 =$ _____

j. $50 \div 5 =$ _____

Use the pictures to solve the problems.

③ Aunt Julie has bought a box of apples. If she puts the apples equally into 5 baskets, how many apples are there in each basket?

_____ = _____   _____ apples

④ Mrs. Brown uses 4 eggs to make an egg dessert. How many egg desserts can she make with a box of eggs?

_____ = _____   _____ egg desserts

⑤ If Lisa cuts a roll of ribbon into 4 pieces of equal length, how long will each piece be?

_____ = _____   _____ m

⑥ Mrs. Welch has a pack of stickers.

a. If she gives her stickers to 4 children with each having the same number of stickers, how many stickers will each child get?

_____ = _____

_____ stickers

b. If Mrs. Welch gives her stickers to 5 children instead, how many stickers will each child get?

_____

= _____

_____ stickers

Did you know?

The rarest seal is the **Mediterranean Monk Seal**, with fewer than 400 left in the world.

Day

47

Dividing by 6 or 7

There are 4 groups in all.

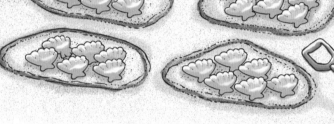

I've collected 24 shells. I put 6 shells in each group.

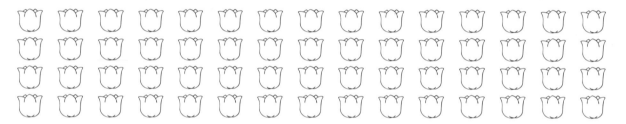

Circle the things into groups. Then do the division.

① a.   Circle every 6 flowers.

b.   6 ÷ 6 = _____   c.   12 ÷ 6 = _____   d.   18 ÷ 6 = _____

e.   24 ÷ 6 = _____   f.   30 ÷ 6 = _____   g.   36 ÷ 6 = _____

h.   42 ÷ 6 = _____   i.   48 ÷ 6 = _____   j.   54 ÷ 6 = _____

② a.   Circle every 7 ants.

b.   7 ÷ 7 = _____   c.   14 ÷ 7 = _____   d.   21 ÷ 7 = _____

e.   28 ÷ 7 = _____   f.   35 ÷ 7 = _____   g.   42 ÷ 7 = _____

h.   49 ÷ 7 = _____   i.   56 ÷ 7 = _____   j.   63 ÷ 7 = _____

Solve the problems.

③ There are 24 children in Mrs. Stanley's class. If Mrs. Stanley divides the children equally into 6 groups, how many children are there in each group?

_____ children

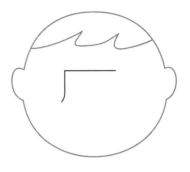

Do you remember there are 7 days in a week?

1 week = 7 days

④ How many weeks are there in 56 days?

_____ weeks

⑤ Aunt Yvonne has baked 48 cupcakes. If each box holds 6 cupcakes, how many boxes does she need to hold all her cupcakes?

_____ boxes

⑥ If each cooler holds 6 boxes of juice, how many coolers are needed for 36 boxes of juice?

_____ coolers

⑦ There are 63 chocolate bars in a box. If Edmond shares a box of chocolate bars with 6 boys, how many chocolate bars will each boy get?

_____ chocolate bars

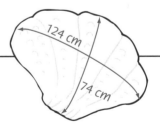

Did you know?

The world's largest **clam** was collected in Australia in 1917. It measured 124 cm by 74 cm, and weighed 263 kg.

124 cm

74 cm

DATE: _____

Day **48**

Dividing by 8 or 9

I need 6 boxes to hold 54 cars.

$54 \div 9 = 6$

Do the division.

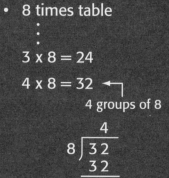

e.g.

$8\overline{)32}$

Think:
- How many groups of 8 are there in 32?
- 8 times table
  ⋮
  $3 \times 8 = 24$
  $4 \times 8 = 32$ ←

  4 groups of 8

$$8\overline{)\begin{array}{c} 4 \\ 32 \\ \underline{32} \end{array}}$$

$32 \div 8 = 4$

① $9\overline{)36}$

② $8\overline{)40}$

③ $9\overline{)81}$

④ $16 \div 8 =$ _____

⑤ $56 \div 8 =$ _____

⑥ $63 \div 9 =$ _____

⑦ $48 \div 8 =$ _____

⑧ $8 \div 8 =$ _____

⑨ $72 \div 9 =$ _____

⑩ **Help Lily do the division to find her dog.**

E $32 \div 8$ = _____

F $72 \div 8$ = _____

A $64 \div 8$ = _____

D $27 \div 9$ = _____

B $18 \div 9$ = _____

C $40 \div 8$ = _____

G $9 \div 9$ = _____

Solve the problems.

⑪

a. How many boxes are needed to hold 56 chocolates?

_____ = _____   _____ boxes

b. How many boxes are needed to hold 32 chocolates?

_____ = _____   _____ boxes

⑫

a. How many stands are needed to hold 72 lollipops?

_____ = _____   _____ stands

b. How many stands are needed to hold 27 lollipops?

_____ = _____   _____ stands

⑬

a. If there are 16 children, how many groups will there be?

_____ = _____   _____ groups

b. If there are 64 children, how many groups will there be?

_____ = _____   _____ groups

For question ⑭, you have to find the total number of children first.

⑭ There are 16 girls and 29 boys in the park. If Mrs. Stein divides the children into groups of 9, how many groups are there in all?

_____

= _____

_____ groups

Did you know?

The most valuable **model car** is a 1937 delivery truck. It was sold for £12 650 in London in 1994.

Day 49

Solving Problems Involving Division

Each group has 8 🍃.

Each group has 9 🌰.

24 🍃 – 3 groups
18 🌰 – 2 groups
36 🥜 – 4 groups

Find and write the answers in the correct boxes to see how many pine cones there are in each box.

①
A 12 ÷ 4   **B** 15 ÷ 3
C 18 ÷ 6   **D** 27 ÷ 9
E 32 ÷ 8   **F** 49 ÷ 7
G 56 ÷ 8   **H** 40 ÷ 5
I 24 ÷ 4   **J** 20 ÷ 4

Solve the problems.

② Elaine has 15 rings. If she puts the rings equally into 5 boxes, there will be _____ rings in each box.

③ Mrs. Welch divides 54 children equally into 6 groups. There are _____ children in each group.

④ There are 4 bottles of juice in a pack. If David wants to buy 32 bottles of juice, he needs to buy _____ packs of juice.

⑤ A roll of ribbon is 56 cm long. If Judy cuts it into 8 pieces of equal length, each piece will be _____ cm long.

Complete the table. Then answer the questions.

⑥

	Containers	Number of Containers Needed
a.  24 pieces		24 ÷ 3 =
	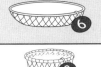 6 pcs	
	 8 pcs	
b.  Potatoes 36	4	
	6	
	9	

⑦ If Diana buys a tin of cookies and shares it with her 3 friends, how many cookies will each child get?

_____ cookies

⑧ If Aunt Betty bakes 6 potatoes each time, how many times will it take her to bake a bag of potatoes?

_____ times

⑨ Mrs. Winter has a big basket of potatoes. If she divides the potatoes equally into 3 portions and gives 1 portion to Lily, how many potatoes will Lily get?

_____ potatoes

Day
50

More about Division

But which of the two ways do you want to make your necklace?

I want each of my necklace to have the same number of beads.

14 ÷ 2 = 7

2 necklaces with 7 beads each

14 ÷ 7 = 2

7 necklaces with 2 beads each

Circle the pictures to match the division sentences.

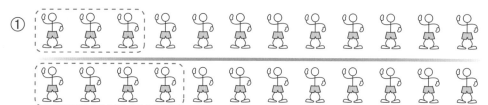

① $12 \div 3 =$ _____

$12 \div 4 =$ _____

② $10 \div 2 =$ _____

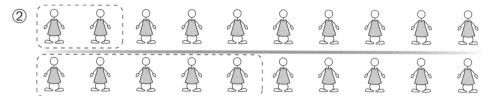

$10 \div 5 =$ _____

③ $15 \div 3 =$ _____

$15 \div 5 =$ _____

Fill in the missing numbers with the help of the given division sentences.

④ $24 \div 3 = 8$

$24 \div$ _____ $= 3$

⑤ $16 \div 8 = 2$

_____ $\div 2 = 8$

⑥ $20 \div 4 = 5$

$20 \div$ _____ $= 4$

⑦ $56 \div 8 = 7$

_____ $\div 7 = 8$

⑧ $54 \div 6 = 9$

$54 \div$ _____ $= 6$

⑨ $35 \div 5 = 7$

_____ $\div 7 = 5$

Read what the children say. Help them solve the problems.

⑩ I have 45 treats. If I put the treats equally into 5 boxes, there will be _____ treats in each box. If I put the treats equally into 9 boxes instead, there will be _____ treats in each box.

⑪ If I buy 9 marbles every month, it will take _____ months for me to have 63 marbles. If I buy 7 marbles every month instead, it will take me _____ months to have 63 marbles.

⑫ I have 35 cookies. If I pack them equally into 7 boxes, there will be _____ cookies in each box. If I repack them into bags of 5 cookies each, how many bags will I need?

_____ bags

⑬ There are 25 brown eggs and 11 white eggs in the basket. If I put the eggs equally into 9 bags, there will be _____ eggs in each bag. If I put them into 4 bags instead, how many eggs will there be in each bag?

_____ eggs

For question ⑬, you have to find the total number of eggs first.

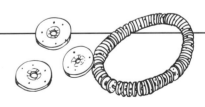

Did you know?

The question of the **oldest beads** is still in dispute, but the oldest beads in Africa were made of Ostrich eggshell. They have been dated to about 40 000 years ago.

Division with Remainders (1)

$$2\overline{)15} \quad \begin{array}{r} 7\,R\,1 \\ \underline{14} \\ 1 \end{array}$$

left over

Circle the correct number of items.
Then do the division.

① In groups of 6

25 ÷ 6 = _____

② In groups of 4

19 ÷ 4 = _____

Do the division.

③ $6\overline{)35}$ 　5R☐

④ $4\overline{)21}$ 　5R☐

⑤ $8\overline{)45}$

⑥ $7\overline{)18}$

⑦ 50 ÷ 9 = _____

⑧ 22 ÷ 3 = _____

⑨ 16 ÷ 5 = _____

⑩ 34 ÷ 6 = _____

e.g. $7\overline{)30}$

Think:
- How many groups of 7 are there in 30?
- 7 times table
  ⋮
  3 x 7 = 21
  4 x 7 = 28 ← closest to and smaller than 30
  5 x 7 = 35

$$7\overline{)30} \quad \begin{array}{r} 4\,R\,2 \\ \underline{28} \\ 2 \end{array}$$
remainder

30 ÷ 7 = 4R2

Solve the problems.

⑪ Winnie has 45 crayons. If she puts them into 6 boxes, how many crayons are there in each box? How many are left?

_____ = _____

There are ____ crayons in each box; ____ crayons are left.

⑫ A plate can hold 5 lemons. How many plates are needed to hold 23 lemons? How many are left?

_____ = _____

____ plates are needed; ____ lemons are left.

⑬ If 8 children share a box of 42 stickers, how many stickers will each child get? How many are left?

_____ = _____

Each child will get ____ stickers; ____ stickers are left.

⑭

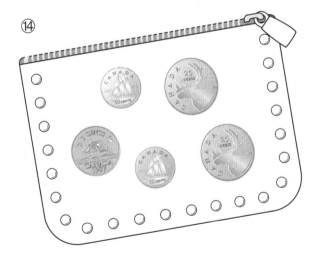

Each lollipop costs 9¢. If Lucy buys her friend some lollipops, how many lollipops can she buy with all her money? How much will be left?

_____ = _____

She can buy ____ lollipops with ____¢ left.

Did you know?

'Cupcakes' were so called because they were originally baked in cups and the ingredients were measured in cups too.

Day 52

Division with Remainders (2)

We need 1 more box to hold the remaining cheesesticks.

Do the division.

①

$$8\overline{)73}$$

②

$$5\overline{)42}$$

③

$$9\overline{)68}$$

④

$$7\overline{)29}$$

⑤ $37 \div 4 =$ _____

⑥ $52 \div 6 =$ _____

⑦ $34 \div 5 =$ _____

⑧ $23 \div 9 =$ _____

⑨ $26 \div 3 =$ _____

⑩ $46 \div 7 =$ _____

Circle the correct number of items. Then fill in the blanks.

⑪ Each box can hold 5 rings.

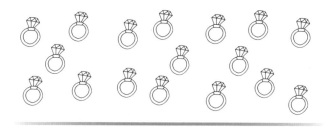

$17 \div 5 =$ _____

_____ boxes are needed to hold 17 rings.

⑫ Each bag can hold 3 fish.

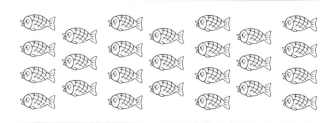

$25 \div 3 =$ _____

_____ bags are needed to hold 25 fish.

Fill in the missing numbers.

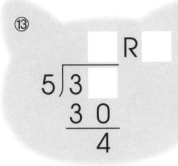

⑬
```
      R
  5)3
  3 0
    4
```

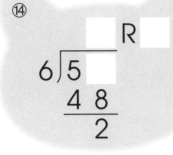

⑭
```
      R
  6)5
  4 8
    2
```

⑮
```
    7 R
  )3
  2 8
    3
```

Solve the problems.

⑯ Aunt Betty has made 45 sandwiches. If she puts 6 sandwiches into a box, how many boxes will she need to hold all the sandwiches?

_____ = _____

She will need _____ boxes.

⑰ A taxi can take 4 passengers. If Mrs. Stanley wants to take 17 children to the Art Centre, how many taxis will they need?

_____ = _____

They will need _____ taxis.

⑱ There are 3 boxes of juice in each pack. If John needs 29 boxes of juice, how many packs of juice should he buy?

_____ = _____

He should buy _____ packs of juice.

⑲ A battery lasts 9 hours. If Dr. Minz wants to do an experiment with a flashlight for a day, how many batteries will he need?

_____ = _____

He will need _____ batteries.

Did you know?

Mice cannot see colours. They see things in shades from black to white.

DATE: _____

Day

53 REVIEW

Use the pictures to find the answers.

①

a.   5 x 8 = _____

b.   40 ÷ 5 = _____

②

a.   6 x 5 = _____

b.   30 ÷ 6 = _____

③

a.   3 x 7 = _____

b.   21 ÷ 3 = _____

Find the answers.

④
```
    3
x   9
```

⑤
```
    6
x   4
```

⑥
```
    9
x   5
```

⑦
```
    7
x   8
```

⑧   6)54

⑨   8)34

⑩   2)18

⑪   9)82

⑫   4 x 7 = _____

⑬   6 x 3 = _____

⑭   16 ÷ 5 = _____

⑮   33 ÷ 4 = _____

⑯   5 x 4 = _____

⑰   2 x 6 = _____

⑱   15 ÷ 9 = _____

⑲   7 x 7 = _____

⑳   35 ÷ 5 = _____

Record the mass of each item. Then answer the questions.

$2 each

Candies

CHIPS 50 g / 400 g

$3 each

chocolate 50 g / 100 g / 10 g

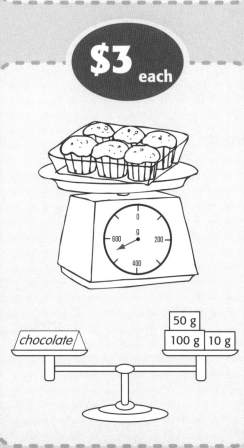

㉑ a. 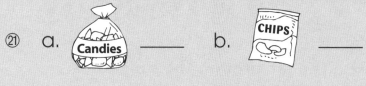 Candies _____   b. CHIPS _____

c. chocolate _____   d. 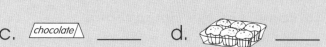 _____

㉒ If Aunt Mary buys the children some candies, how many bags of candies can she buy with $16?

_____ = _____

She can buy _____ bags.

㉓ If Willie buys 7 bags of chips, how much does he need to pay?

_____ = _____

He needs to pay $ _____ .

㉔ How much do 9 chocolate bars cost?

_____ = _____

They cost $ _____ .

㉕ Uncle Ted needs 40 muffins. How many boxes of muffins does he need to buy?

_____ = _____

He needs to buy _____ boxes.

YOU Deserve A Break!

Use the pictures on the sunglasses to complete the times table.

①

X	2	5
1		
2		
3		
4		
5		
6		
7		
8		
9		

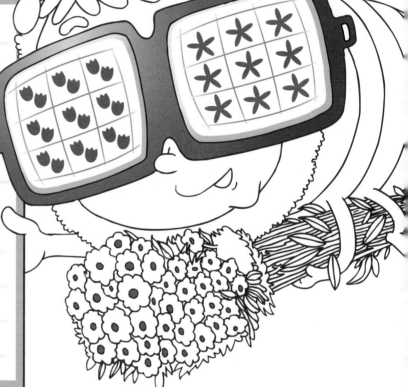

Look at the flowers Ben Bee is holding. Help him do the division.

② 4 ⟌ 39

③ 5 ⟌ 39

④ 6 ⟌ 39

⑤ 7 ⟌ 39

⑥ 39 ÷ 8 = _____

⑦ 39 ÷ 9 = _____

Use the flowers to find the answers.

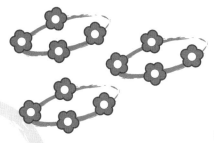

⑧

a. 3 x 4 = _____

b. 12 ÷ 3 = _____

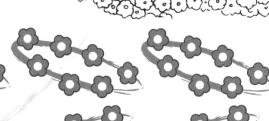

⑨ a. 5 x 7 = _____

b. 35 ÷ 5 = _____

Read what the bees say. Help them solve the problems.

⑩

It takes me 2 hours to collect a bucket of honey; it takes me _____ hours to collect 8 buckets of honey.

⑪

A bucket of honey can fill up 16 cups. If 4 bees share a bucket of honey, each bee can get _____ cups of honey.

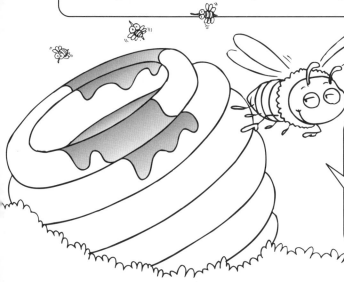

⑫

Each box can hold 5 pots of honey. _____ boxes are needed to hold 39 pots.

Divisibility of 2, 5, or 10

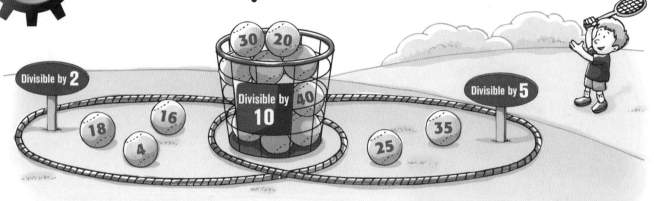

Colour the numbers that are divisible by 2.

①

6   28   55

39   10

81   63   18

24   47

52   86

A number is divisible by 2 if its ones digit is even.

e.g.

Tens	Ones
1	**4**

← 4 is an even number.

14 is divisible by 2.

A number is divisible by 5 if its ones digit is 0 or 5.

e.g.

Tens	Ones
4	**5**

← 5 is at the ones place.

45 is divisible by 5.

A number is divisible by 10 if its ones digit is 0.

e.g.

Tens	Ones
5	**0**

← 0 is at the ones place.

50 is divisible by 10.

② **Tim has to go through the numbers that are divisible by 5. Draw a line to show Tim the path to get his trophy.**

16   15

66

90   28   50

55   24   77

32   64

84   20   81

60   23

18   65

40

35

39

45

75   22   33   80

Do the division if the numbers are divisible by 10.

③ **A** $10\overline{)50}$ **B** $10\overline{)34}$ **C** $10\overline{)40}$ **D** $10\overline{)16}$

E 30 ÷ 10 = _____   **F** 72 ÷ 10 = _____   **G** 29 ÷ 10 = _____

H 61 ÷ 10 = _____   **I** 60 ÷ 10 = _____   **J** 80 ÷ 10 = _____

Circle the numbers that are divisible by each pair of given numbers.

④
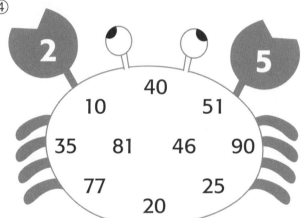

2   5
40
10   51
35   81   46   90
77   25
20

⑤
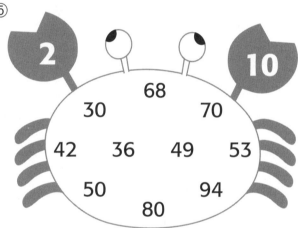

2   10
68
30   70
42   36   49   53
50   94
80

Answer the children's questions.

⑥  *What numbers between 361 and 369 are divisible by 2?*

_____

⑦   *What numbers between 424 and 443 are divisible by 5?*

_____

⑧  *What numbers between 845 and 876 are divisible by 10?*

_____

DATE: _____

Two-step Problems

No. of fruits:

```
    6
  + 8
   14
```

```
    7
2 ) 1 4
    1 4
```

Let's share them. Each of us gets 7.

Solve the problems.

① There are 14 green apples and 58 red apples. If Judy divides the apples into 9 groups, how many apples will there be in each group?

Total number of apples : _____ + _____ = _____

Number of apples in each group: _____ ÷ _____ = _____

② Henry has 60 marbles. After giving 4 marbles to his brother, Henry puts his marbles into 7 bags, how many marbles are there in each bag?

Number of marbles left: _____ = _____

Number of marbles in each bag: _____ = _____

③ There are 4 carnations and 5 roses in a bunch. If Mr. Stanley buys 7 bunches of flowers, how many flowers will he have?

Number of flowers in a bunch: _____ = _____

Number of flowers Mr. Stanley will have: _____ = _____

Look at the pictures. Solve the problems. Show your work.

④ Mr. White has bought 4 boxes of pizzas. If he puts every 2 pizzas on a plate, how many plates does he need to hold all the pizzas?

He needs _____ plates.

⑤ Mabel has bought 4 cakes and cut them into slices of equal size. If her guests eat 25 slices of cakes, how many slices of cakes will be left?

_____ slices of cakes will be left.

⑥ Helen has a box of candies. If she gives 9 candies to her brother and then shares the rest with 7 girls, how many candies will each girl get?

Each girl will get _____ candies.

⑦ Joe has 4 $5 bills. If Joe buys a top, how much will he have left?

Did you know?

Steps are built to bridge a large vertical distance by dividing it into smaller ones.

He will have $ _____ left.

DATE: _____

Day **57**

Relating Multiplication and Division

A Fact Family

3 x 4 = 12
4 x 3 = 12
12 ÷ 3 = 4
12 ÷ 4 = 3

Complete the number sentences to match the pictures in each group.

①

5 x 6 = _____

6 x _____ = 30

30 ÷ 5 = _____

30 ÷ _____ = 5

②

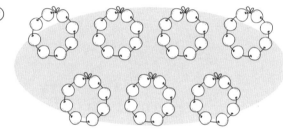

7 x 8 = _____

8 x _____ = 56

56 ÷ 7 = _____

_____ ÷ 8 = 7

③

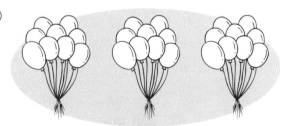

3 x _____ = _____

9 x _____ = 27

27 ÷ _____ = _____

_____ ÷ 3 = _____

④

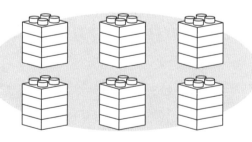

4 x _____ = _____

6 x _____ = 24

24 ÷ _____ = _____

_____ ÷ _____ = 4

Choose any 3 numbers in each group to write a multiplication and a division sentence.

⑤ 9 15 6 54

_____ X _____ = _____

_____ ÷ _____ = _____

⑥ 35 7 2 5

_____ X _____ = _____

_____ ÷ _____ = _____

⑦ 16 2 4 8

_____ X _____ = _____

_____ ÷ _____ = _____

⑧ 5 4 9 36

_____ X _____ = _____

_____ ÷ _____ = _____

 Fill in the blanks with the help of the given number sentences.

⑨ 15 x 8 = 120

120 ÷ 15 = _____

⑩ 9 x 36 = 324

324 ÷ 36 = _____

⑫ 96 ÷ 4 = 24

_____ x 4 = 96

⑪ 115 ÷ 23 = 5

5 x 23 = _____

⑬ 7 x 🍎 = 🍊

🍊 ÷ 7 = _____

⑭ ♡ x ☆ = 🍃

🍃 ÷ ♡ = _____

Fractions (1)

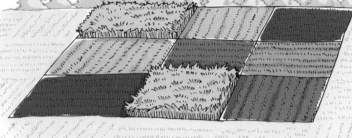

$\frac{2}{9}$ of the fields are planted with wheat.

e.g.
- 8 equal parts
- 3 parts shaded

$\frac{3}{8}$ of the rectangle is shaded.

Trace the dotted lines and colour the correct number of parts. Then write fractions to tell how many parts are coloured.

①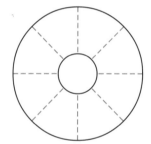

Colour 2 parts;

_____ is coloured.

②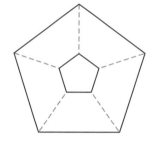

Colour 3 parts;

_____ is coloured.

③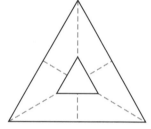

Colour 2 parts;

_____ is coloured.

Trace the dotted lines to put the things in groups and colour the correct number of groups. Then write fractions to tell how many groups are coloured.

④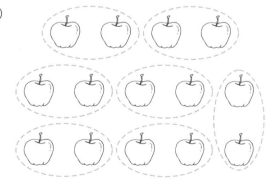

Colour 2 groups; _____ of the apples are coloured.

⑤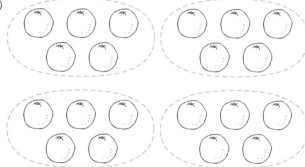

Colour 3 groups; _____ of the oranges are coloured.

Colour the figures to show the fractions. Then put ' < ' or ' > ' in the circles.

⑥ $\dfrac{7}{8}$ ◯ $\dfrac{6}{8}$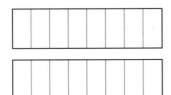

⑦ $\dfrac{5}{9}$ ◯ $\dfrac{2}{9}$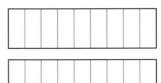

⑧ $\dfrac{4}{5}$ ◯ $\dfrac{2}{3}$

⑨ $\dfrac{3}{8}$ ◯ $\dfrac{5}{6}$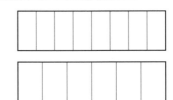

See how the children group their stickers. Help them solve the problems.

⑩

Look at my stickers, how many groups of stickers do I have?

Joe

_____ groups

⑪ What fraction of Joe's stickers are letters? _____

⑫ What fraction of Joe's stickers are bees? _____

⑬ *Look at my stickers, how many groups of stickers do I have?*

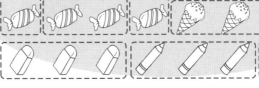

_____ groups

Sally

⑭ What fraction of Sally's stickers are candies?

_____

⑮ What fraction of Sally's stickers are stationery items?

_____

Did you know?

Wheat is the second largest cereal crop after corn. Rice comes third.

DATE:

Fractions (2)

I have $2\frac{5}{8}$ boxes of rings.

Write the fractions for the things shown.

①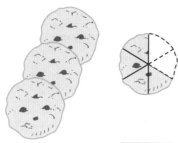

_____

②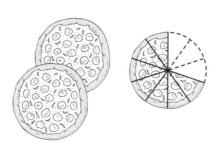

_____

> A mixed number is formed by a whole number and a fraction.
>
> e.g.
>
> 2 wholes $\frac{1}{4}$
>
> $2\frac{1}{4}$ of the circles are shaded.

③

_____

④

_____

Colour the rectangles to show the fractions and cross out X any unused rectangles.

⑤ $2\frac{4}{5}$

⑥ $3\frac{2}{3}$

⑦ $1\frac{3}{8}$

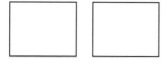

Comparing mixed numbers:

1st Compare the whole number parts. If they are the same, go to **2nd** .

2nd Compare the fraction parts.

e.g. $3\frac{4}{5}$ $3\frac{2}{5}$

They are the same.

$3\frac{4}{5}$ $3\frac{2}{5}$

$\frac{4}{5} > \frac{2}{5}$

$3\frac{4}{5} > 3\frac{2}{5}$

Circle the greater mixed number in each group.

⑧ $2\frac{1}{8}$ $3\frac{3}{4}$ ⑨ $1\frac{1}{5}$ $2\frac{3}{5}$

⑩ $4\frac{2}{7}$ $2\frac{4}{7}$ ⑪ $3\frac{7}{9}$ $3\frac{1}{9}$

⑫ $1\frac{7}{10}$ $7\frac{1}{10}$ ⑬ $4\frac{1}{4}$ $5\frac{1}{4}$

⑭ $2\frac{3}{8}$ $1\frac{7}{8}$ ⑮ $5\frac{5}{6}$ $6\frac{1}{6}$

Look at the pictures and read what the people say. Help them fill in the blanks with fractions to complete the sentences.

⑯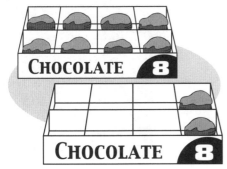

I have 2 boxes of chocolate. After giving my friends some chocolates, I still have some left.

Kevin

Kevin gives his friends _____ box of chocolates; he has _____ boxes of chocolates left.

⑰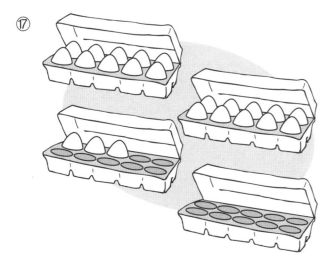

I had 4 cartons of eggs. I've used some eggs to make cakes.

Mrs. Stanley

Mrs. Stanley used _____ cartons of eggs to make cakes; she has _____ cartons of eggs left.

Shapes (1)

Draw the missing side of each shape. Then sort them by letters.

①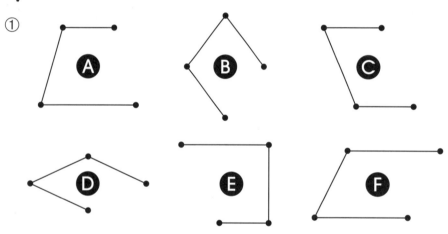

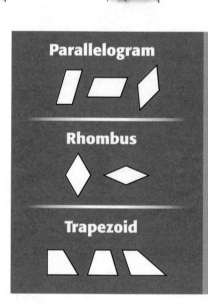

Parallelogram

Rhombus

Trapezoid

Parallelogram	Rhombus	Trapezoid

Look at the picture. Count and write the number of shapes.

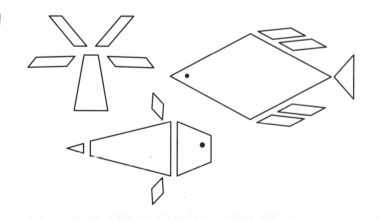

② Parallelogram: _____

　 Rhombus: _____

　 Trapezoid: _____

　 Triangle: _____

Draw the shapes.

③ 3 different rhombuses

④ 3 different parallelograms

⑤ 3 different trapezoids

Colour the sides and circle the vertices of each shape with a red pencil. Then complete the table.

⑥

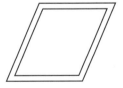
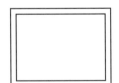

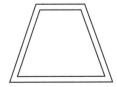

	No. of Sides	No. of Vertices
Parallelogram		
Rectangle		
Rhombus		
Square		
Trapezoid		
Triangle		

Day
61

Shapes (2)

You broke my square.

No, we are making a rhombus.

Check ✔ the shapes that can be built with each group of sticks.

4 sticks of the same length:

 or

A **square** or a **rhombus** can be built with 4 sticks of the same length.

① | | |

Ⓐ Parallelogram

Ⓑ Rhombus

Ⓒ Triangle

② | | | |

Ⓐ Parallelogram   Ⓑ Trapezoid

Ⓒ Rhombus   Ⓓ Rectangle

③ | | V | |

Ⓐ Square   Ⓑ Trapezoid

Ⓒ Triangle   Ⓓ Parallelogram

If you cut each shape along the dotted lines, what shapes will you get? Write the answers.

④

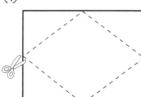

• ____ rhombus

• ____ triangles

⑤

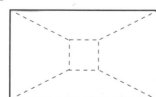

• _____

• _____

Read what the children say. Draw lines on the shapes to show how to cut each shape.

⑥

I want to get 1 parallelogram and 2 triangles from a rectangle.

⑦

How can I get 4 parallelograms from a rhombus?

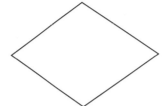

⑧

How can I get 1 rectangle and 2 triangles from a parallelogram?

⑨

How can I get 3 triangles from this trapezoid?

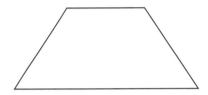

Measure and record the sides of the shapes. Then check ✔ the correct sentences.

⑩

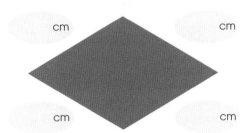

cm cm cm cm

cm cm cm cm

⑪ A rhombus has 4 equal sides. ◯

⑫ A parallelogram has no equal sides. ◯

⑬ The opposite sides of a parallelogram are equal. ◯

Did you know?

Parallelogram

Squares, rectangles, and rhombuses are also parallelograms.

DATE: _____

Congruent and Similar Shapes

Congruent Shapes:
- same size and shape

e.g.

Similar Shapes:
- same shape but different sizes

e.g.

Tell whether each pair of pictures is congruent or similar. Write `congruent´ or `similar´ on the line.

① **A**    **B**   **C**

D    **E**    **F**

A _____   **B** _____   **C** _____

D _____   **E** _____   **F** _____

Draw a shape that is congruent to each given shape.

② 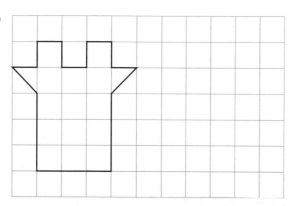   ③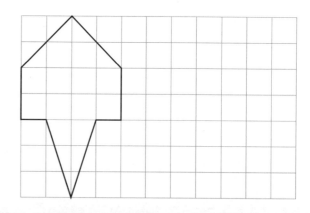

Colour the shapes that are similar to the given shapes.

④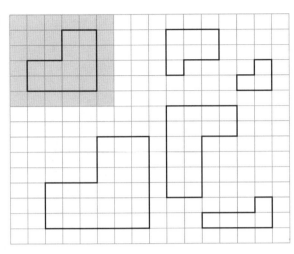

⑤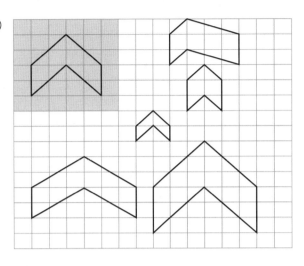

Measure the sides of the shapes. Then tell whether the shapes in each pair are congruent or similar. Write `congruent´ or `similar´ on the lines.

⑥

⑦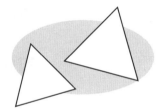

⑧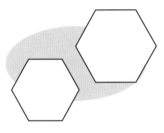

_____

_____

_____

Trace the shapes to see how to make pictures with congruent and similar shapes.

⑨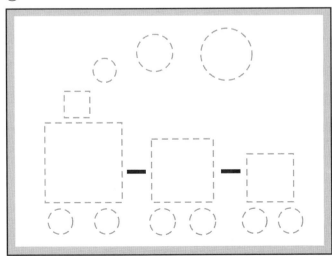

⑩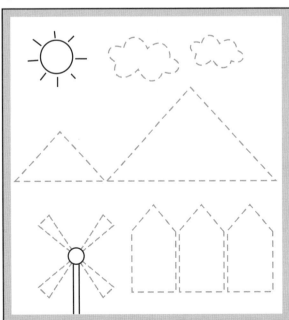

Day
63

Tile Patterns

Colour the ones that are tile patterns. Then name the shapes of the tiles.

Tile Patterns:

- shapes that can cover an area without gaps or overlaps

e.g.

Not Tile Pattern	Tile Pattern
having gaps	
overlapping each other	

①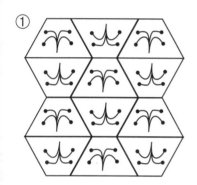

②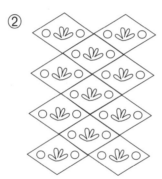

_____

_____

③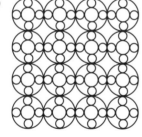

④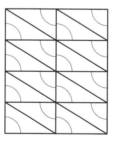

⑤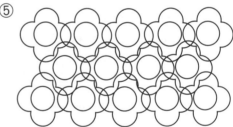

_____

_____

_____

⑥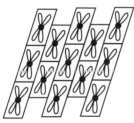

⑦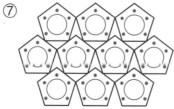

⑧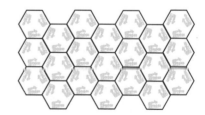

_____

_____

_____

Trace the dotted lines to complete the tile patterns. Then follow the patterns to draw one more column.

⑨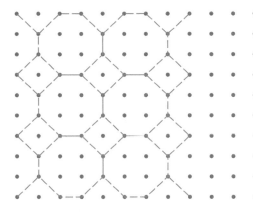

⑩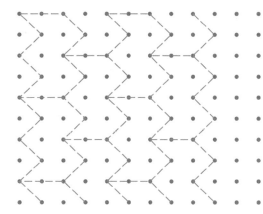

⑪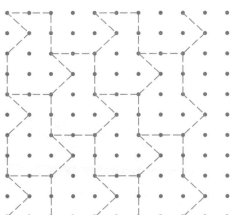

⑫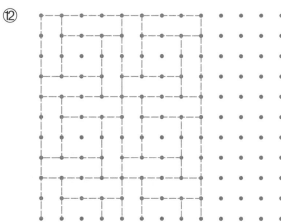

Use the given shapes to create your own patterns.

Ⓐ **Triangle**   **Rhombus**

Ⓑ **Parallelogram**   **Trapezoid**

⑬

DATE: _____

Lines of Symmetry

We have 4 different ways to share this equally because a square has 4 lines of symmetry.

Draw lines of symmetry for the shapes if there is any.

> A **line of symmetry** is a line that cuts a shape in halves. Each side of the shape is exactly the same as the other.
>
> e.g.
>
> has 5 lines of symmetry.

①

②

③

④

⑤

⑥

⑦

Draw lines of symmetry for the shapes. Then write the numbers in the circles.

⑧

A○   B○   C○

The dotted lines are the lines of symmetry of each shape. Draw the missing sides to complete each shape.

⑨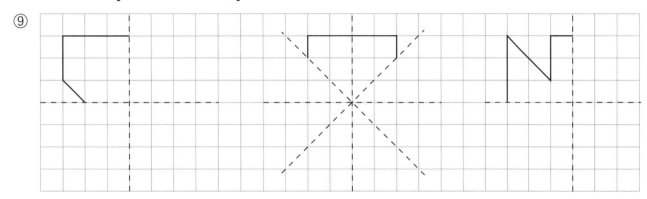

Read what each child says. Put a check mark ✔ in the circle if it is correct; otherwise, put a cross ✘ and correct the underlined number or word to make the sentence true.

⑩ *A square has <u>3</u> lines of symmetry.* ○ _____

⑪ *No matter what size a parallelogram is, it has <u>no</u> lines of symmetry.* ○ _____

⑫ *If a triangle has 2 equal sides, it must have <u>2</u> lines of symmetry.* ○ _____

⑬ *If I get 2 congruent triangles by cutting a rectangle, each triangle has <u>no</u> lines of symmetry.* ○ _____

Triangle	Number of Lines of Symmetry
no sides equal	0
2 sides equal	1
3 sides equal	3

Did you know?

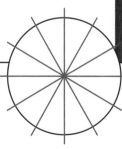

A circle has **many lines of symmetry**, since any line through its centre is a line of symmetry.

Day
65

Naming 3-D Figures

Let's welcome our newcomer, Rectangular Pyramid.

Draw lines to sort the solids by type.

①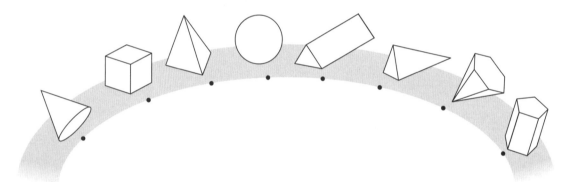

Prism   Pyramid

Name the shape of the base of each prism. Then name the prism.

②   Base: _____

Name of Prism: _____

③   Base: _____

Name of Prism: _____

④   Base: _____

Name of Prism: _____

Prisms are named by the shape of the **bases**.

e.g.

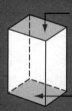

The bases are in the shape of a rectangle.

Name of Prism:
Rectangular prism

Pyramids are named by the shape of the **bases**.

e.g.

The base is in the shape of a rectangle.

Name of Pyramid:
Rectangular pyramid

Name the shape of the base of each pyramid. Then name the pyramid.

A  B   C   D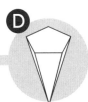

⑤

	Shape of Base	Name of Pyramid
A		
B		
C		
D		

Find out what prisms or pyramids the children are describing. Write their names.

⑥ *It has 1 rectangular face and 4 triangular faces.*

_____

⑦ *It has 2 triangular faces and 3 rectangular faces.*

_____

⑧ *It has 2 hexagonal faces and 6 rectangular faces.*

_____

Did you know?

⑨ *It has 1 pentagonal face and 5 triangular faces.*

_____

The Great Pyramid of Cholula in Mexico is the largest pyramid in the world. Its volume is almost $\frac{1}{3}$ larger than that of the Great Pyramid in Egypt.

Sorting 3-D Figures

Solid With 5 Gems

Solids With 6 Gems

Give me the rectangular pyramid there!

Sort the given solids. Write the letters.

①

With Triangular Faces	Without Triangular Faces

②

With Rectangular Faces	Without Rectangular Faces

③

With 5 or Fewer Faces	With More Than 5 Faces

④

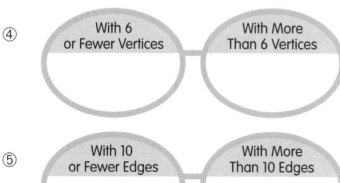

With 6 or Fewer Vertices

With More Than 6 Vertices

⑤

With 10 or Fewer Edges

With More Than 10 Edges

(A) (B) (C) (D) (E) (F)

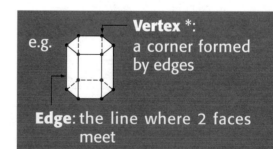

Vertex *:
a corner formed by edges

e.g.

Edge: the line where 2 faces meet

*Vertex (plural: vertices)

Check ✔ the correct answers.

⑥ Which solid has rectangular faces?

Ⓐ Hexagonal pyramid   Ⓑ Triangular prism

Ⓒ Cube

⑦ Which solid has triangular faces?

Ⓐ Pentagonal pyramid   Ⓑ Hexagonal prism

Ⓒ Cylinder

⑧ Which solid has 5 faces?

Ⓐ Triangular pyramid   Ⓑ Hexagonal prism

Ⓒ Rectangular pyramid

⑨ Which solids have 6 vertices?

Ⓐ Rectangular pyramid   Ⓑ Pentagonal pyramid

Ⓒ Triangular prism   Ⓓ Rectangular prism

⑩ Which solids have 12 edges?

Ⓐ Rectangular prism   Ⓑ Triangular pyramid

Ⓒ Rectangular pyramid   Ⓓ Hexagonal pyramid

⑪ *Which solids can have edges that are all equal in length?*

Ⓐ Rectangular pyramid   Ⓑ Cube

Ⓒ Cylinder   Ⓓ Triangular pyramid

When the edges of a triangular pyramid are equal in length, you can call it a **'Tetrahedron'**.

Did you know?

The Crown of Louis XV is the sole surviving crown after the French Revolution. Originally it contained the famous '**Regent**' diamond and hundreds of other gems which had been stolen.

Day **67**

DATE: _____

Constructing 3-D Figures

See how I'm building a square pyramid with 8 sticks and 5 marshmallows.

If you follow the arrows to fold the paper, what 3-D figures will you get? Name them.

①

Ⓐ _____

Ⓑ _____

Ⓒ _____

Ⓓ _____

Ⓔ _____

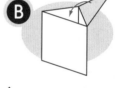
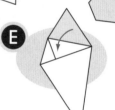

Trace the dotted lines. Then draw the missing parts and fill in the blanks.

②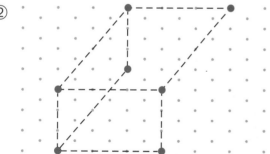

It is a _____ ; it has _____ vertices and _____ edges.

③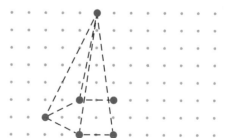

It is a _____ ; it has _____ vertices and _____ edges.

Colour the shapes you need to make a 3-D figure that matches each skeleton.

④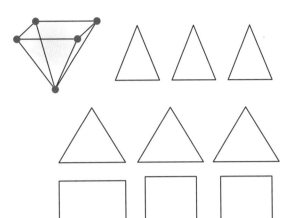

⑤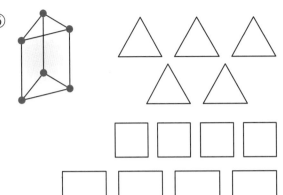

⑥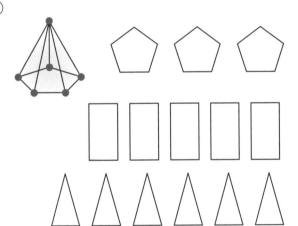

⑦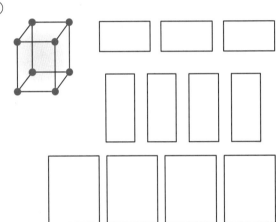

Fill in the blanks.

⑧ Lucy has used 3 long sticks, 6 short sticks, and 6 marshmallows to build a _____ prism.

⑨ Ted has used _____ sticks and _____ marshmallows to build a hexagonal pyramid.

⑩ Marco has used 1 pentagon, _____ triangles, and 6 marshmallows to build a _____ .

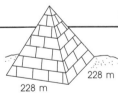

Nets of 3-D Figures

Do you like my rectangular prism?

Look at the net of the rectangular prism. Colour each pair of congruent faces with the same colour. Then fill in the blanks and circle the correct word.

①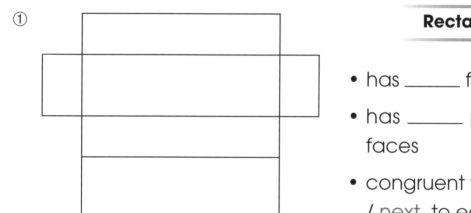

Rectangular Prism

- has _____ faces in all
- has _____ pairs of congruent faces
- congruent faces are opposite / next to each other

Check ✔ the nets that can form a rectangular prism.

②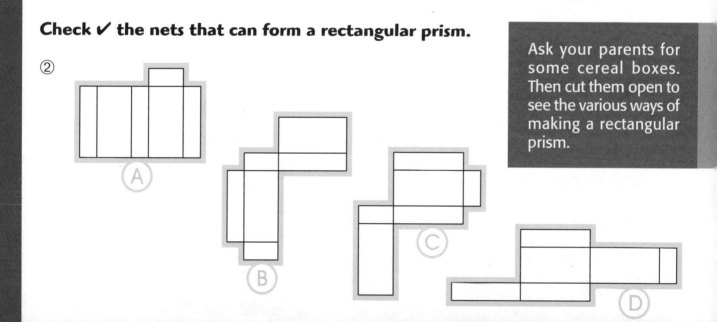

Ⓐ   Ⓑ   Ⓒ   Ⓓ

Ask your parents for some cereal boxes. Then cut them open to see the various ways of making a rectangular prism.

Match the nets with the rectangular prisms.

③

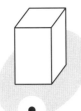 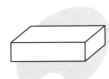 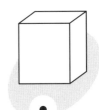

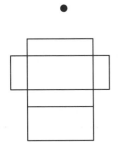 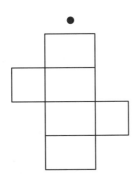 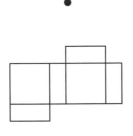 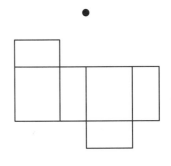

Draw the missing parts of each net of a rectangular prism.

④

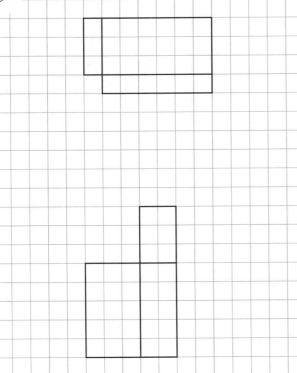 

Day
69

Transformations – Translation

See which pairs of pictures show a translation. Check ✔ the letters.

① Before After

Ⓐ

Before After

Ⓑ

A **translation** is a transformation that moves a figure to a new position. The figure does not change its size, shape, or orientation.

e.g.

translation image

translate

Before After

Ⓒ

Before After

Ⓓ

Before After

Ⓔ

Before After

Ⓕ

Before After

Ⓖ

Draw the translation image of each picture.

②

③

Follow the directions to draw the translation images of the given shapes.

④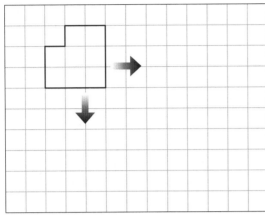

⑤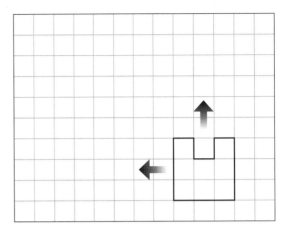

⑥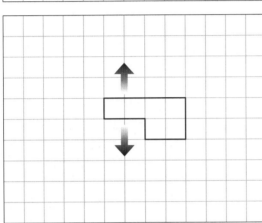

⑦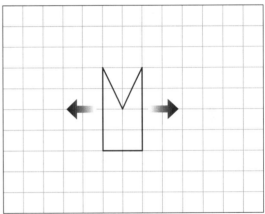

Colour the patterns that are created by translating a single tile.

⑧

A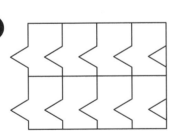

B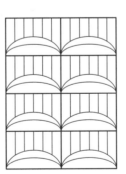

C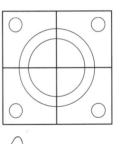

D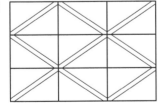

E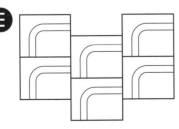

Did you know?

Bowlingual, a dog translator, was invented to translate dog barks into human language in 2002.

Day
70

Transformations – Reflection

Line of Reflection

See which pairs of pictures show a reflection. Check ✔ the letters.

A **reflection** is a transformation that flips a figure over a line. The figure does not change size or shape, but it does change position or orientation.

e.g.
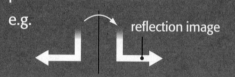
reflection image

① Before → After   Before → After

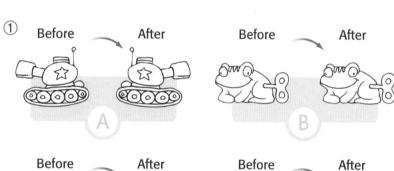
Ⓐ   Ⓑ

Before → After   Before → After   Before → After

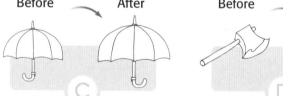 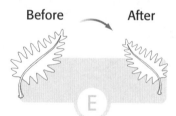
Ⓒ   Ⓓ   Ⓔ

Draw the reflection image of each picture.

②

③

The coloured line is the line of reflection. Complete the reflection image of each picture.

④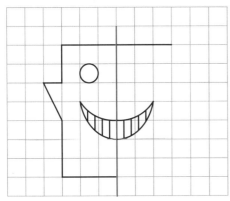

⑤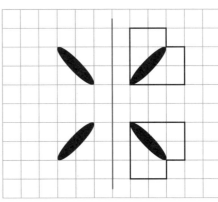

⑥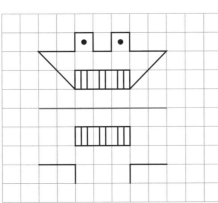

⑦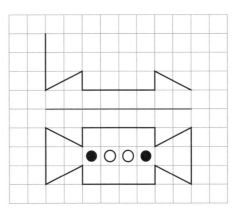

Draw the line of reflection for each pair of pictures. Then draw the missing parts.

⑧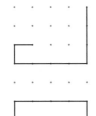

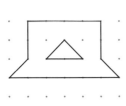 

Did you know?

Leonardo da Vinci is famous for 'mirror writing'. He wrote most of his personal notes as a reflection image to protect his ideas from being stolen.

Circle the correct numbers.

①   Divisible by 2:   Divisible by 5:   Divisible by 2 and 10:

Divisible by 2		Divisible by 5		Divisible by 2 and 10	
56	42	24	50	40	54
34	39	36	20	73	60
27	10	15	85	90	81
18	23	42	37	62	80

Trace the dotted lines to put the things in groups. Then fill in the blanks with fractions to complete the sentences.

②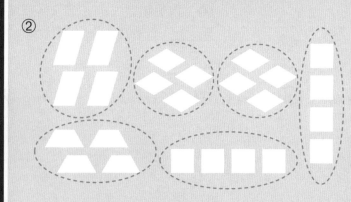

a. _____ of the shapes are rhombuses.

b. _____ of the shapes are parallelograms.

c. _____ of the shapes are squares.

③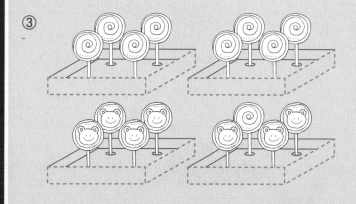

a. _____ boxes of lollipops are 🍭 .

b. _____ boxes of lollipops are 🐸 .

Circle the greater fraction in each group.

④ $\dfrac{5}{9}$ $\dfrac{1}{9}$ ⑤ $\dfrac{3}{7}$ $\dfrac{6}{7}$ ⑥ $1\dfrac{4}{5}$ $2\dfrac{1}{5}$ ⑦ $4\dfrac{5}{8}$ $4\dfrac{1}{8}$

Name the 3-D figures. Then answer the questions with letters.

⑧ Ⓐ _____   Ⓑ _____

   Ⓒ _____   Ⓓ _____

⑨ Which figures have 6 vertices?   _____

⑩ Which figures have triangular faces?   _____

⑪ Which figure is formed by folding

   ?   _____

Draw the image of each picture.

⑫ Translation image

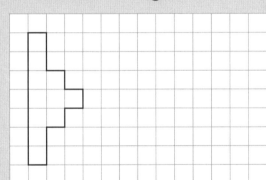

⑬ Reflection image

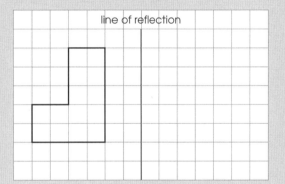

Solve the problems.

⑭ Sabrina has 16 flowers. If she gives 2 flowers to her mother and then divides the rest into 2 groups, how many flowers are there in each group?

   Number of flowers left: _____ = _____

   Number of flowers in each group: _____ = _____

⑮ Each book costs $2. If Sally buys 6 books, she will have $5 left. How much does Sally have?

   Sally has $ _____ .

You Deserve A Break!

The cat will only let the mice go if they can solve the problems on the cards. Solve the problems to help free the mice.

① Draw the lines of symmetry of each shape.

② Complete the tile pattern.

③ Name each solid. Then write the number of marshmallows and sticks needed to build the skeleton of each solid.

a. _____ ; ___ ◯ ___ /

b. _____ ; ___ ◯ ___ /

c. _____ ; ___ ◯ ___ /

⑥ Cindy the Cat has caught 24 mice. If she divides them into 4 groups and gives 2 groups to her friends, how many mice will her friends get?

_____ mice

⑤ Circle the numbers that are divisible by:

a.
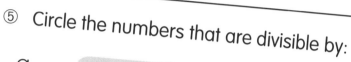

2   9   25   46   62
    18   33   57

b.

5 & 10   40   25   84   95
    32   17   60   30

④ Circle every two identical letters to put the letters in groups. Then fill in the blanks with fractions.

AA AA AA AA
BB BB BB CC

_____ of the groups are 'A';

_____ are 'B' and _____

are 'C'.

DATE: _____

Transformations – Rotation (1)

A quarter turn

Colour each pair of pictures that show a rotation.

> A **rotation** is a transformation that turns a figure about a fixed point. The figure does not change in size or in shape, but it does change position and orientation.
>
> e.g.
>
> turn centre

① Before   After

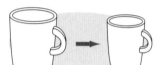

② Before   After

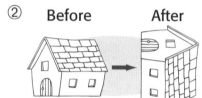

③ Before   After

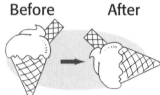

④ Before   After

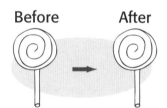

⑤ Before   After

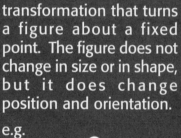

⑥ Before   After

⑦ Before   After

In each picture, which is the image after a quarter turn? Circle it.

⑧

⑨

In each picture, which is the image after a half turn? Circle it.

⑩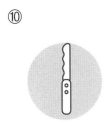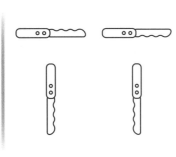

⑪

In each picture, which is the image after a three-quarter turn? Circle it.

⑫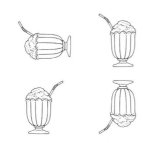

⑬

Draw lines to tell how each picture can be rotated in the counter-clockwise direction.

⑭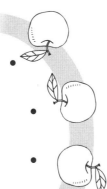

A quarter turn •

A half turn •

A three-quarter turn •

⑮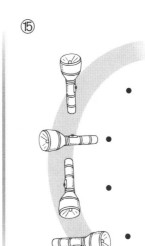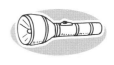

• A quarter turn

• A half turn

• A three-quarter turn

Turning in a counter-clockwise direction ↺ :
e.g.
a quarter turn

Did you know?

Tango is originated in Argentina. The **Argentine Tango** is danced counter-clockwise around the outside of the dance floor.

Transformations – Rotation (2)

- $\frac{1}{4}$ turn clockwise
- $\frac{1}{2}$ turn clockwise
- $\frac{1}{4}$ turn counter-clockwise

Draw the missing part of each rotation image.

①

②

③

④

⑤

⑥

Put a cross X in each picture to show the turn centre of each rotation. Then circle the correct fraction to tell how the picture is rotated.

⑦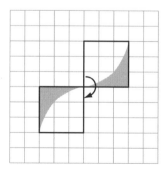

⑧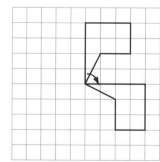

⑨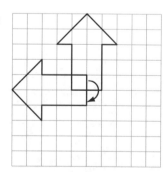

A $\frac{1}{4}$ $\frac{1}{2}$ $\frac{3}{4}$ turn   A $\frac{1}{4}$ $\frac{1}{2}$ $\frac{3}{4}$ turn   A $\frac{1}{4}$ $\frac{1}{2}$ $\frac{3}{4}$ turn

The · is the turn centre. Complete the rotation images. Then write 'quarter', 'half', or 'three-quarter' to tell how each shape is rotated.

⑩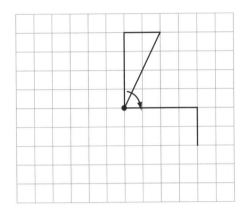

A _____ turn

⑪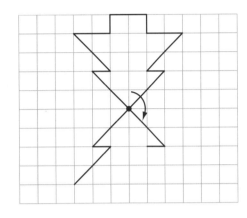

A _____ turn

⑫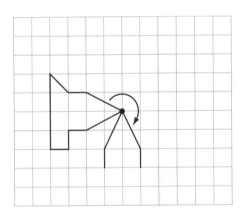

A _____ turn

⑬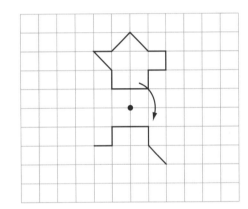

A _____ turn

Answer Lucy's question.

⑭

If I make a three-quarter turn of a picture in the clockwise direction, the image will be the same as the one after a quarter turn counter-clockwise. Am I correct?

_____

Did you know?

The **largest bank vault door** in the world is found in the Federal Reserve Bank of Cleveland in Ohio, U.S. It is about $1\frac{1}{2}$ m thick.

More about Transformations

Write 'Translation', 'Reflection', or 'Rotation'.

①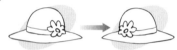

_____

②

_____

③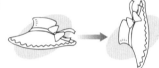

_____

④

_____

⑤

_____

⑥

_____

For each picture, draw an image for each transformation.

	Translation	Reflection	Rotation
⑦ 			
⑧ 			

For each shape, find the correct transformed images. Write 'Translation', 'Reflection', or 'Rotation' on the line.

⑨

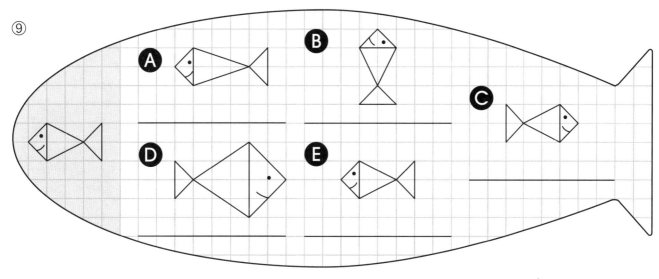

⑩

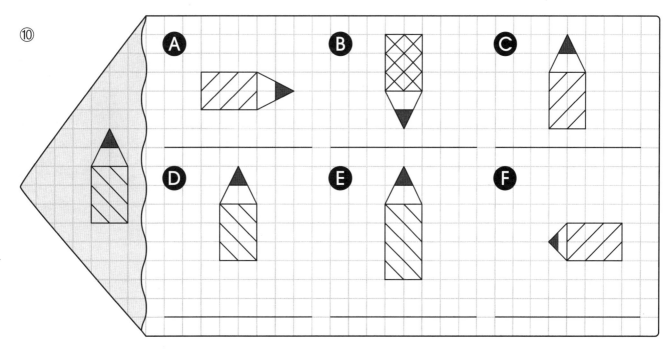

Draw the translation, reflection, and rotation images of the striped triangle.

⑪

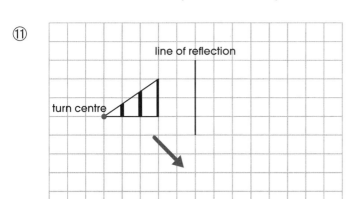
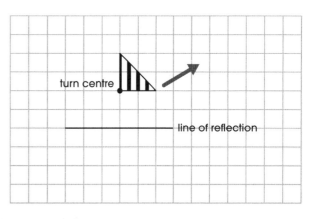

Coordinates (1)

They are at B3, D2, and G1.

Look at the grid. Fill in the blanks. Then write the coordinates of the animals.

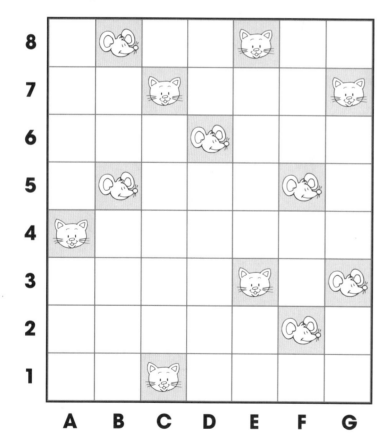

Using letters and numbers to locate a point on a grid:

1st Write the letter.

2nd Write the number.

♥ is at B3.

③

_____ _____

_____ _____

_____ _____

_____ _____

_____ _____

_____ _____

① There are _____ columns on this grid. They are from _____ to _____ .

② There are _____ rows on this grid. They are from _____ to _____ .

Draw the pictures on the grid. Then answer the questions.

④

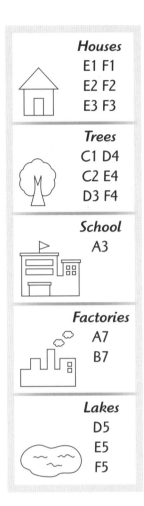

Houses	
E1	F1
E2	F2
E3	F3

Trees
C1	D4
C2	E4
D3	F4

School
A3

Factories
A7
B7

Lakes
D5
E5
F5

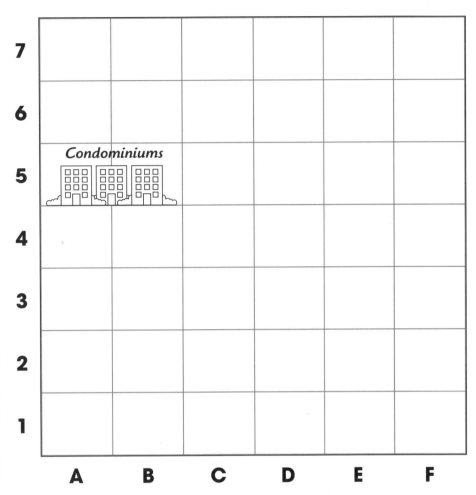

⑤ Which house is farthest from the factories? Colour it yellow.

⑥ Which house is nearest to the school? Colour it blue.

⑦ There is a bridge connecting A5 and C7. Draw the bridge on the grid.

⑧ What are the locations of the condominiums?

_____

⑨ Jason's father, Mr. Smith, wants to move to a place that is closest to the school and the factories. Give him a suggestion.

_____

Did you know?

Since at least 3500 years ago, Ancient Egyptians used **cats** to keep mice away from their grain. Cats were even mummified after they died.

Coordinates (2)

The treasure chest is 3 squares right and 2 squares up from our boat.

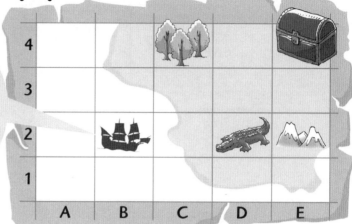

Write the missing letters and numbers to complete the grid. Then do the questions to help the children find their favourite animals.

①

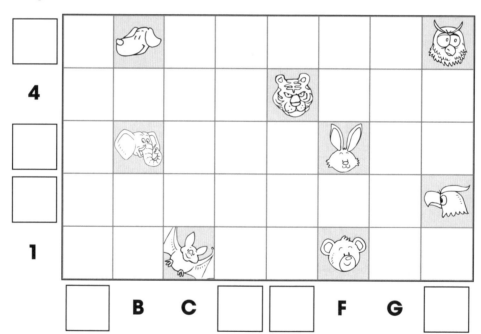

②　Judy's favourite animal is 2 squares down from the dog. Which animal is it? What is its location?

_____ ;

_____

③　Leon's favourite animal is 2 squares left and 1 square up from the parrot. Which animal is it? What is its location?

_____ ;

_____

④　Ted is at C1. If he goes 2 squares right and 3 squares up, he will find his favourite animal. Which one is his favourite animal? What is its location?

_____ ;

_____

Write the missing letters and numbers to complete the grid. Then solve the problems.

⑤

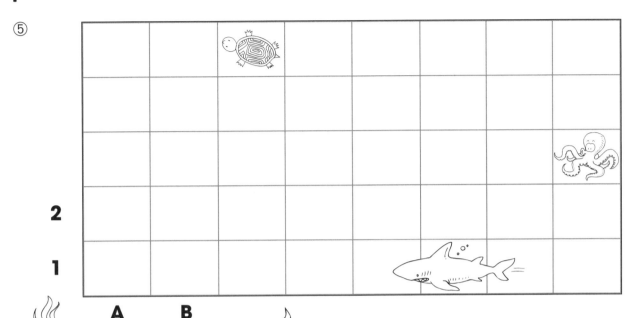

2

1

    A   **B**

⑥ The fish are at A3, B5, C1, C2, D5, F4, and G4. Draw them on the grid.

⑦ If the octopus wants to catch the closest fish, he should go _____ square(s) left / right and _____ square(s) up / down .

⑧ If the shark goes 2 squares left and then 1 square up, it can eat _____ fish along the way. Their coordinates are _____ .

⑨ If the turtle goes 2 squares left and then 2 squares down, it can eat _____ fish along the way. Their coordinates are _____ .

⑩ There is a shrimp at C3. If it goes 2 squares right and 2 squares down, will it bump into the shark?

_____

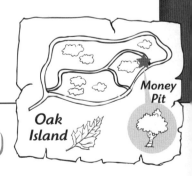

Did you know?

Money Pit

Oak Island

Oak Island is located off the eastern coast of Nova Scotia, Canada. It is well known as the Money Pit, where pirates had buried their treasures.

DATE: _____

Identifying Patterns

This pattern is created by changing colour and position.

Is it my turn yet?

Find out which two attributes change in each pattern. Fill in the blanks with the given words.

colour

orientation

pattern

position

shape

size

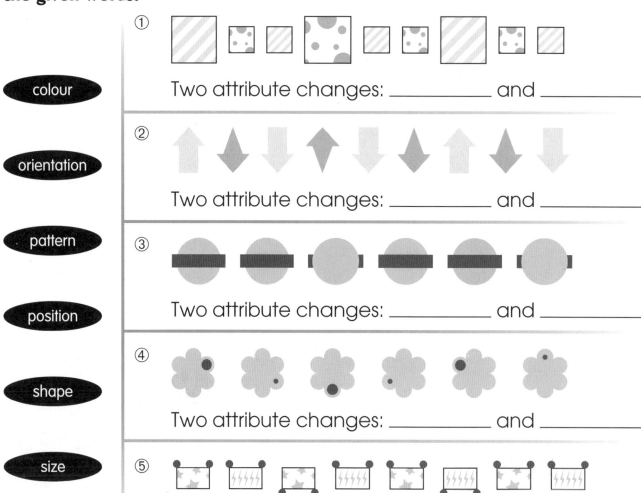

① Two attribute changes: _____ and _____

② Two attribute changes: _____ and _____

③ Two attribute changes: _____ and _____

④ Two attribute changes: _____ and _____

⑤ Two attribute changes: _____ and _____

Find out the two attribute changes in each pattern. Then draw the next two pictures and describe the pattern by using the given words.

⑥

a.

b. Shape of face (round, square):

round, _____ , _____ , _____

c. Size of eye (big, small):

big, _____ , _____

⑦

a.

b. Orientation of arrow (left, right):

_____

c. Pattern of arrow (dots, stripes):

_____

⑧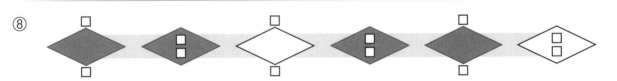

a.

b. Position of square (inside, outside):

_____

c. Colour of rhombus (grey, white):

_____

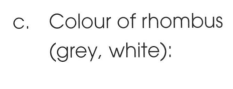

Did you know?

The world's largest cardboard box was made in Toronto in 2001. The box can hold about 240 000 cans of pop.

240 000 pop

Creating Patterns

> *I've created a pattern by changing size and colour.*

Follow the instructions to colour or draw shapes in the given patterns. Then write the two attribute changes in the patterns.

① Colour the heart: blue, yellow, green

Attribute changes: _____ and _____

② Draw a square: above the heart, under the heart, under the heart

Attribute changes: _____ and _____

③ Draw an arrow inside each circle: pointing upwards, pointing downwards, pointing downwards

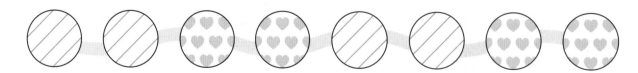

Attribute changes: _____ and _____

Find the attribute changes in each pattern. Then use the same elements to create a pattern that is different from the one given.

④

⑤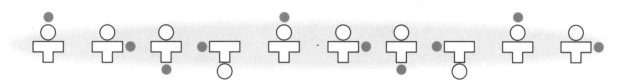

Draw the missing pictures.

⑥ 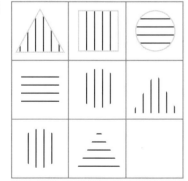   ⑦ 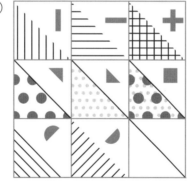   ⑧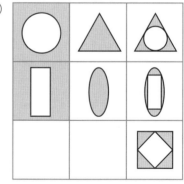

⑨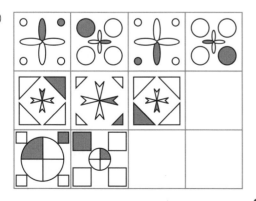

Did you know?

The longest snake ever found was a **reticulated python** in Indonesia in 1912. It was about 10 m long.

Day
80

Number Patterns

Put 3 ornaments on the first layer; then put 3 more on each layer each time.

4th layer

1st layer

2nd layer

3rd layer

Follow each pattern rule. Fill in the missing numbers.

① **+ 4**   4   8   12   16   ____ ____   28   ____ ____

② **− 5**   90   85   ____   75   ____ ____   60   55   ____

③ **− 8** / **+ 3**

80   75   ____   ____   65   60
      72   67   ____   ____   ____

④ **x 2** / **− 1**

2   3   ____   ____   ____
      4   6   10   ____   34

Read each pattern rule. Write the next three numbers for each pattern.

⑤ Plus 4, minus 3   85 89 86 90 ____ ____ ____

⑥ Minus 10, plus 2   76 66 68 58 ____ ____ ____

⑦ Plus 6, plus 5   19 25 30 36 ____ ____ ____

Look for the number pattern and fill in the missing numbers.

⑧
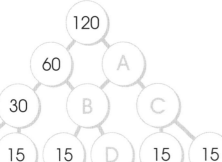

120
60   A
30   B   C
15   15   15   D   15   15

⑨

64   14   36   A   28   18
   50   25   B
      C   15
         D

Read what the children say. Complete the tables to show the patterns and solve the problems.

⑩ I ate 5 cherries on Monday, 9 on Tuesday, 13 on Wednesday, and 17 on Thursday. Following this pattern, how many cherries did I eat on Friday?

a.
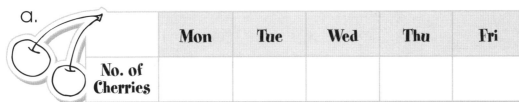

	Mon	Tue	Wed	Thu	Fri
No. of Cherries					

Joanne

b.   How many cherries did Joanne eat in all from Monday to Friday?

_____ cherries

⑪ If I lost 3 toy cars in January, 6 in February, 9 in March, and 12 in April, how many toy cars would I lose in May?

Paul

a.

No. of Lost Cars

Jan	Feb	Mar	Apr	May

b.   How many toy cars would Paul lose in June?

_____ cars

Did you know?

The largest **Christmas bauble ornament** in the world was made in Mexico in 2000. It was made of steel and plastic with a diameter of more than 4 m.

Patterns in a Hundreds Chart

> I coloured some of the numbers in the chart while I was skip-counting by 4's.

Do the multiplication. Then use red to colour the answers in the chart and solve the problems.

① 7 x 1 = _____

7 x 2 = _____

7 x 3 = _____

7 x 4 = _____

7 x 5 = _____

7 x 6 = _____

7 x 7 = _____

7 x 8 = _____

7 x 9 = _____

7 x 10 = _____

1	2	3	4	5	6	7	8	9	10
11	12	13	14	15	16	17	18	19	20
21	22	23	24	25	26	27	28	29	30
31	32	33	34	35	36	37	38	39	40
41	42	43	44	45	46	47	48	49	50
51	52	53	54	55	56	57	58	59	60
61	62	63	64	65	66	67	68	69	70
71	72	73	74	75	76	77	78	79	80
81	82	83	84	85	86	87	88	89	90
91	92	93	94	95	96	97	98	99	100

② Continue the pattern of the numbers in red by using yellow to colour the next four numbers.

③ a. 7 x 11 = _____   b. 7 x 12 = _____

c. 7 x 13 = _____   d. 7 x 14 = _____

For question ③, you can use the yellow numbers to find the answers.

Look at the circled and the coloured numbers in the number sentences. Colour them in the chart. Then follow the patterns to find the missing answers.

1	2	3	4	5	6	7	8	9	10
11	12	13	14	15	16	17	18	19	20
21	22	23	24	25	26	27	28	29	30
31	32	33	34	35	36	37	38	39	40
41	42	43	44	45	46	47	48	49	50
51	52	53	54	55	56	57	58	59	60
61	62	63	64	65	66	67	68	69	70
71	72	73	74	75	76	77	78	79	80
81	82	83	84	85	86	87	88	89	90
91	92	93	94	95	96	97	98	99	100

④ a. (31) – 9 = 22

   (32) – 9 = 23

   (33) – 9 = 24

   (34) – 9 = 25

   (35) – 9 = 26

   b. 37 – 9 = _____

   _____ – 9 = 29

⑤ a. (73) + 8 +10 = 91

   (74) + 8 +10 = 92

   (75) + 8 +10 = 93

   (76) + 8 +10 = 94

   (77) + 8 +10 = 95

   b. 79 + 8 +10 = _____

   _____ + 8 +10 = 98

Use the chart above to fill in the missing numbers.

⑥ a. 22 + 9 = _____

   b. 23 + 9 = _____

⑦ a. 95 – 8 – 10 = _____

   b. 94 – 8 – 10 = _____

Did you know?

The world's **largest box of chocolates** was made in Chicago in 2002. It weighed 1463 kg!

DATE:

Reading Pictographs

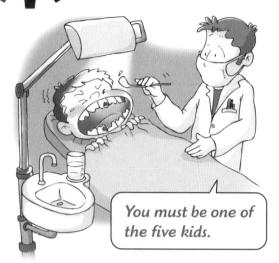

You must be one of the five kids.

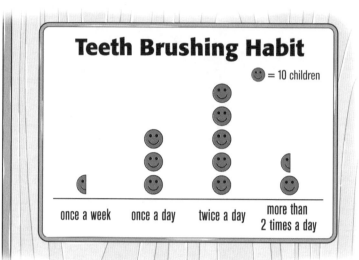

Teeth Brushing Habit

😊 = 10 children

once a week   once a day   twice a day   more than 2 times a day

Read the graph showing the number of people who visited Dr. Milne's office in the past few months. Then answer the questions.

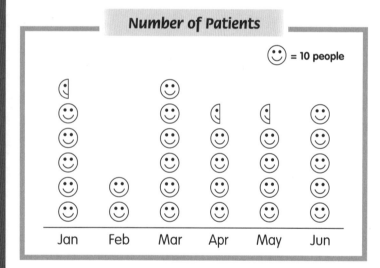

Number of Patients

😊 = 10 people

Jan   Feb   Mar   Apr   May   Jun

When you read a pictograph, remember to check the legend to see how many items each picture represents.

Half of a picture stands for half the number represented by a whole picture.

e.g. = 10   = 5

① How many people does ◖ represent? _____ people

② How many people visited Dr. Milne in January? _____ people

③ Which month is the busiest? _____

④ Which two months have the same number of patients? _____

⑤ Dr. Milne had a 2-week vacation within the past 6 months. Which month did he have the vacation? Explain.

_____

Read the graph showing the number of boxes of toothpaste ordered by different stores. Then complete the table and fill in the blanks.

Number of Boxes of Toothpaste Ordered

 = 100 boxes

Grace's Superstore   K&M Convenience Store   Lucy's Drug Mart   Uncle Bill's Mart

⑥

	Grace's Superstore	K&M Convenience Store	Lucy's Drug Mart	Uncle Bill's Mart
No. of Boxes of Toothpaste Ordered				

⑦ If there are 8 tubes of toothpaste in a box, Grace's Superstore has ordered _____ tubes of toothpaste in all.

⑧ K&M Convenience Store has ordered _____ more boxes of toothpaste than Lucy's Drug Mart.

⑨ If Uncle Bill's Mart sells 50 boxes of toothpaste every month, it will take _____ months to sell all the toothpaste in this order.

Did you know?

Human grows 2 sets of **teeth**. Children have 20 milk teeth, while the permanent set is formed between the ages of 6 and 12.

Making Pictographs

5 chicks hatched this Friday morning.

No. of Chicks Hatched

= 10 eggs

Mon Tue Wed Thu Fri

Uncle Jim and his friends have collected some gold coins. Help them make a pictograph to show the data. Then answer the questions.

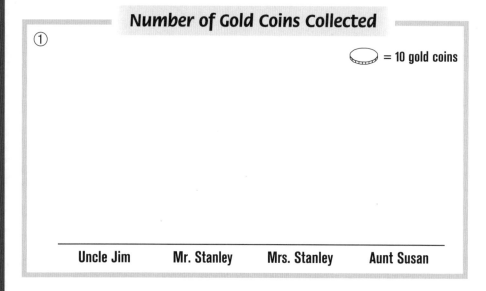

Number of Gold Coins Collected

① = 10 gold coins

Uncle Jim   Mr. Stanley   Mrs. Stanley   Aunt Susan

Number of Gold Coins	
Uncle Jim	**45**
Mr. Stanley	**30**
Mrs. Stanley	**40**
Aunt Susan	**25**

② What is the title of this graph? _____

③ How many gold coins does each picture represent? _____ gold coins

④ How many gold coins do the Stanleys have? _____ gold coins

⑤ Who has the most gold coins? _____

⑥ If Aunt Susan wants to have the same number of gold coins as Uncle Jim, how many gold coins does she need to buy? _____ gold coins

Read the table to see how many bags of chocolate eggs were sold last week. Then complete the pictograph and answer the questions.

⑦

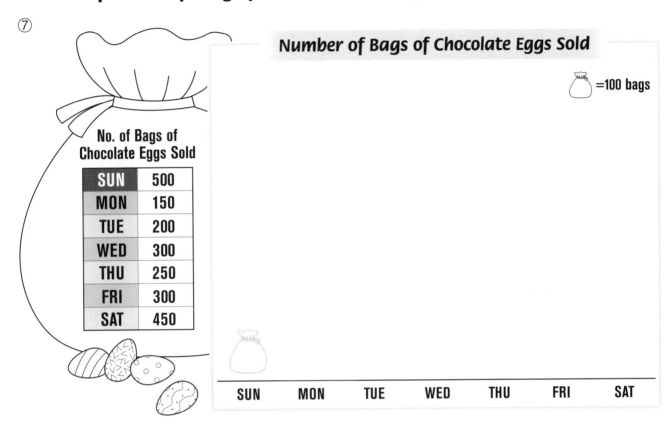

No. of Bags of Chocolate Eggs Sold

SUN	500
MON	150
TUE	200
WED	300
THU	250
FRI	300
SAT	450

Number of Bags of Chocolate Eggs Sold

= 100 bags

SUN   MON   TUE   WED   THU   FRI   SAT

⑧ What is the title of the graph? _____

⑨ How many bags of chocolate eggs were sold on Monday and Tuesday combined? _____ bags

⑩ How many bags of chocolate eggs were sold during the weekend? _____ bags

⑪ Which day had the most chocolate eggs sold? Suggest why most of the chocolate eggs were sold that day.

_____

⑫ If each bag of chocolate eggs cost $1, how much was received from selling the chocolate eggs last week?

$ _____

Did you know?

The tallest **chocolate Easter egg** was made in Belgium in 2005. It was more than 8 m tall.

DATE:

Day **84**

Reading Bar Graphs

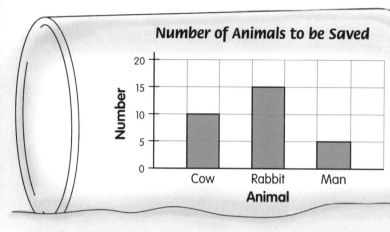

Number of Animals to be Saved

Read the graph showing the sale of sandwiches yesterday. Then complete the table and answer the questions.

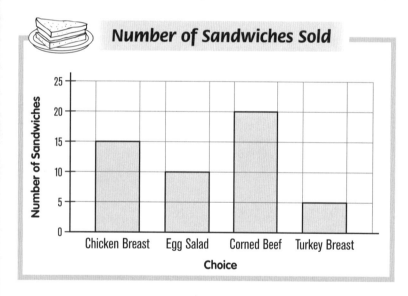

Number of Sandwiches Sold

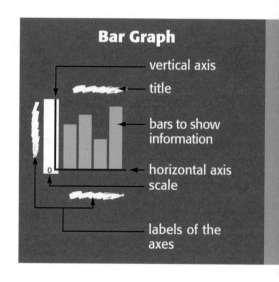

Bar Graph

- vertical axis
- title
- bars to show information
- horizontal axis
- scale
- labels of the axes

① Title of the graph: _____

② Label of the vertical axis: _____

③ Label of the horizontal axis: _____

④ There were ___ choices of sandwiches; they were _____

_____ .

⑤ ___ chicken breast sandwiches were sold.

⑥ ___ sandwiches were sold in all.

The children have made a bar graph to show the number of storybooks collected.
Use the graph to complete the table and answer the questions.

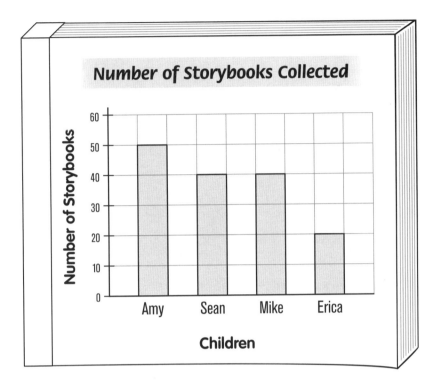

⑦

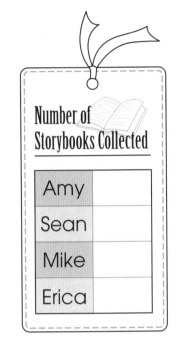

Number of Storybooks Collected

Amy	
Sean	
Mike	
Erica	

⑧ What is the title of the graph? _____

⑨ Which two children have the same number of storybooks?

_____ and _____

⑩ How many storybooks do the girls have in all?

_____ storybooks

⑪ How many storybooks do the boys have in all?

_____ storybooks

⑫ How many storybooks do the children have in all?

_____ storybooks

⑬ How many storybooks does Amy need to give Sean if they want to have the same number of storybooks?

_____ storybooks

Did you know?

3 cm

The world's smallest **wine bottles** were only about 3 cm tall. They were hand-blown in U.S. in 1999.

DATE: _____

Making Bar Graphs

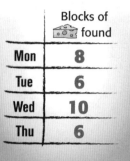

	Blocks of 🧀 found
Mon	8
Tue	6
Wed	10
Thu	6

Blocks of Cheese Found

See what kind of food the children in Mrs. Stanley's class have for lunch. Help them complete the bar graph to show the data. Then answer the questions.

① **What the Children Have for Lunch**

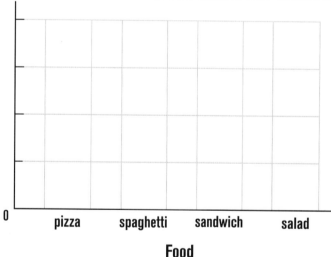

Number of Children (vertical axis)

pizza   spaghetti   sandwich   salad

Food

Food	Number of Children
Pizza	4
Spaghetti	8
Sandwich	6
Salad	6

② What is the label of the vertical axis?

_____

③ Most of the children have _____ for lunch.

④ There are _____ children in Mrs. Stanley's class.

First look at the data. Then see what scale should be used to present them.

I think the scale of this graph should be in multiples of 2.

See how many combos were sold yesterday. Help Uncle Ray round the numbers to the nearest ten. Then use the rounded figures to complete the bar graph and answer the questions.

⑤ —— Number of Combos Sold ——

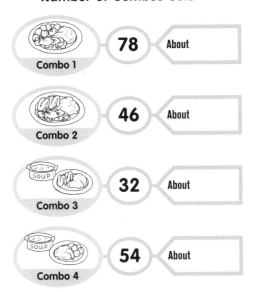

Combo 1 — 78 — About

Combo 2 — 46 — About

Combo 3 — 32 — About

Combo 4 — 54 — About

Number of Combos Sold

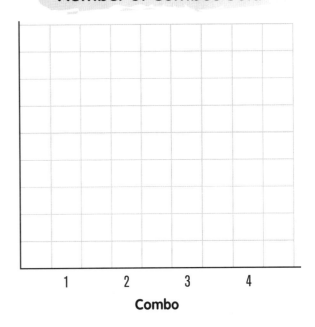

Number of Combos

Combo

⑥ What is the title of the graph? _____

⑦ What is the label of the horizontal axis? _____

⑧ About how many Combo 1's and Combo 2's were sold in all?   _____ combos

⑨ About how many more Combo 4's were sold than Combo 3's?   _____ more

⑩ About how many combos were sold in all yesterday?

_____ combos

⑪ If Uncle Ray wants to cut one of the combos from his menu, which one should it be? Explain.

_____

_____

Did you know?

The **largest cheese** in the world weighed over 26 000 kg. It was made in Quebec in 1995.

Circle Graphs

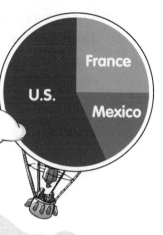

Favourite
Vacation Destinations

France

U.S.

Mexico

*Most people want
to visit the U.S.*

**Aunt Sally has made a circle graph to show
the kinds of flowers sold in her shop yesterday.
Use the circle graph to answer the questions.**

Kinds of Flowers Sold

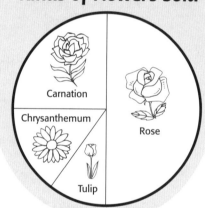

① What is the title of this graph?

_____

② How many kinds of flowers are there
in Aunt Sally's flower shop? What are
they?

_____

_____

③ Which kind of flower was sold the most?   _____

④ Which kind of flower was sold the least?   _____

⑤ Which kind of flower was a bit less popular
than the carnation?   _____

⑥ If Aunt Sally wants to replace one kind of flower with a new one,
which do you think she should replace? Why?

_____

Read what Dr. Bell says. Help him label each section on the circle graph. Then answer the questions.

I spent most of my time doing the 'Apollo' experiment yesterday. The time that I spent doing the 'Lotus' experiment was a bit less than the time I spent on 'Apollo'. My assistant had a day off yesterday, so I had to work on the 'A & B' experiment myself. Fortunately, I spent the least time on that one.

Time Spent on Different Experiments

⑦

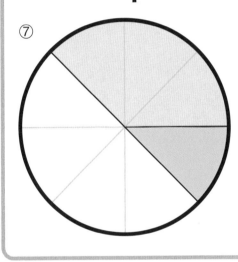

⑧ If Dr. Bell works 8 hours a day, how many hours of work would each section on the circle graph represent?

_____ hour(s)

⑨ If each section on the graph represents 1 hour, how many hours would Dr. Bell spend on each experiment?

'Apollo': _____ h   'Lotus': _____ h

'A & B': _____ h

⑩ Which experiment took half of Dr. Bell's time yesterday?

_____

⑪ If Dr. Bell makes a circle graph to show the time he spends on each experiment today, will the circle graph be the same as the one above? Explain.

_____

_____

_____

_____

BREITLING ORBITER 3

Did you know?

In 1999, a **manned balloon** circumnavigatted the globe in 21 days. It set the balloon travelling distance record of 40 814 km.

Probability (1)

You'll have a greater chance of getting a bear this time.

Read the description of each block. Then help the children solve the problems.

① The numbers on this block are from 1 to 6.

If Lillian rolls this block once,

   a.   what are the numbers she could get?

        _____

   b.   does she have any chances of getting a number greater than 6?   _____

   c.   are the chances of getting a '1' or a '3' the same?   _____

② The letters on this block are from A to F.

If Robert rolls this block once,

   a.   what are the letters he could get?

        _____

   b.   does he have any chances of getting a 'M'?   _____

   c.   are there any chances of getting A and F at the same time?   _____

Look at the things that the children have. Answer the questions.

③

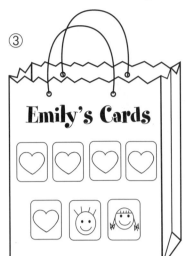

If Emily lets Tim draw 1 card from her bag,

a. what are the cards Tim could get?

_____

b. will Tim have a greater chance of getting a or a ☺ ? _____

c. will Tim have a smaller chance of getting a ♡ or a 👧 ? _____

④

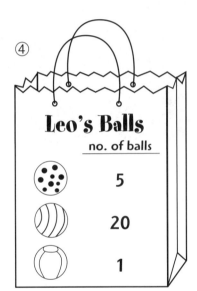

George is going to draw a ball from Leo's bag.

a. What are the possible outcomes?

_____

b. Are the chances of drawing a 🔵 or a 🏐 the same? _____

c. Which ball is least likely to be drawn? _____

⑤

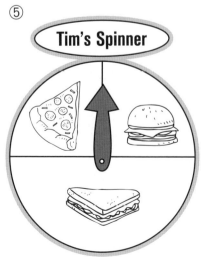

Ada is going to spin Tim's spinner once.

a. What food could the spinner land on?

_____

b. Is there any chance of landing on a 🌭 ? _____

c. Are the chances of landing on a 🍕 , 🍔 , or 🥪 the same? _____

Probability (2)

It doesn't matter how hard you shake it; there's a greater chance of getting a than a ⭐ anyway.

Choose the best words to describe the chances of each event.

Unlikely   Likely

Impossible

Certain

I will see many tulips in winter.

That's impossible.

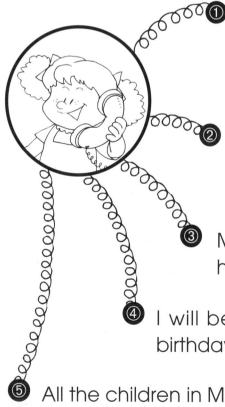

① My uncle will buy a car after he passes the driving test.   _____

② My mom has a day off on Saturday. She will take me to see a movie.   _____

③ My friends will give me a house on my birthday.   _____

④ I will be a year older on my next birthday.   _____

⑤ All the children in Mrs. Venn's class will get more than full marks on the next test.   _____

Christie has a spinner and wants to spin it 40 times to see where the arrow will land each time. Help her predict the results by putting a check mark ✔ in the circles for the correct sentences. Then answer the questions.

⑥

a. The arrow has the greatest chance of landing on 'Candy'. ◯

b. The arrow has the least chance of landing on 'Gum'. ◯

c. The arrow has a greater chance of landing on 'Candy' than on 'Sorry!'. ◯

d. The arrow is less likely to land on 'Gum' than on 'Sorry!'. ◯

e. There is a chance of getting a chocolate bar. ◯

f. The bigger the section, the greater the chance the arrow will land on it. ◯

⑦ Which table best shows Christie's spins? Check ✔ the answer.

Ⓐ
	No. of Times
Gum	25
Candy	5
Sorry!	10

Ⓑ
	No. of Times
Gum	5
Candy	10
Sorry!	25

Ⓒ
	No. of Times
Gum	10
Candy	5
Sorry!	25

⑧ Christie says that if she spins the spinner 100 times, the number of times the arrow lands on 'Sorry!' is about 60. Is she correct?

Did you know?

Marbles were originally made of clay or marble. In 1902, Martin F. Christensen invented the glass-marble-making machine, which automated the marble making process.

Day
89 REVIEW

DATE: _____

Follow each pattern to draw the next two pictures. Then use the given words to tell which two attributes change in each pattern.

colour   orientation   pattern   position   shape   size

①

Two attribute changes: _____ and _____

②

Two attribute changes: _____ and _____

Draw the pictures on the grid. Then answer the questions.

③ 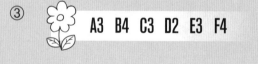 A3 B4 C3 D2 E3 F4   C2 D5 E2 F3

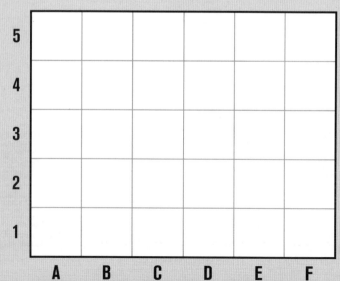

④ If the butterfly at F3 flies to the left, it can see _____ flowers along the way.

⑤ There are no butterflies on columns _____ and _____ .

Complete the rotation images. Then write 'quarter', 'half', or 'three-quarter' on the line to tell how the shape is rotated.

⑥
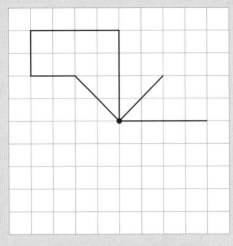

A _____ turn clockwise

⑦
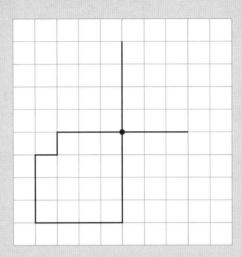

A _____ turn counterclockwise

Use a bar graph to show the same set of data on the pictograph. Then fill in the blanks.

Andrew's Savings  = 10¢

⑧

_____

Money Saved (¢)

50
40
30
20
10
0

Day of the week

⑨ Andrew saved _____ ¢ in all; he was _____ ¢ short of trading for a toonie.

Look at the balls in the box. Write 'impossible', 'unlikely', 'likely', or 'certain' to complete the sentences.

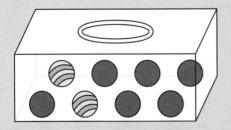

⑩ It is _____ to draw a striped ball.

⑪ It is _____ to draw a letter ball.

⑫ It is _____ to draw a coloured ball.

⑬ It is _____ to draw a ball.

DATE: _____

YOU Deserve A Break!

Which blocks on the grid are covered by the fish and the crab? Write the answers in the boxes. Then complete the pattern on the fish and the graph on the crab.

①

②

	Dad Crab	Mom Crab	Brother Crab	Sister Crab
No. of Fish Caught	15	10	20	5

No. of Fish

20
15
10
5
0

Dad Crab

4 3 2 1

A B C D E

Blocks Covered:

Blocks Covered:

Blocks Covered:

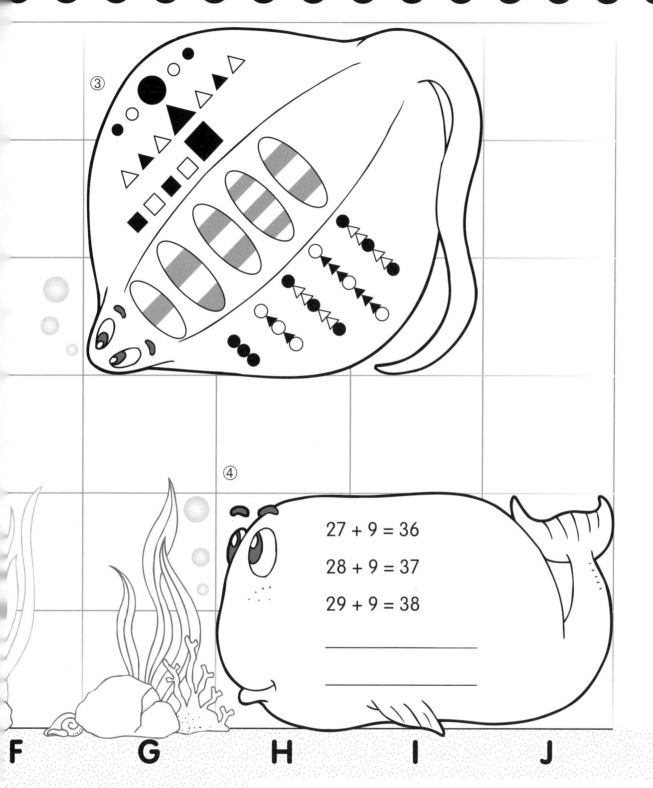

③

④

$$27 + 9 = 36$$

$$28 + 9 = 37$$

$$29 + 9 = 38$$

_____

_____

F　　**G**　　**H**　　**I**　　**J**

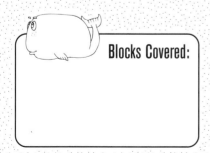

Blocks Covered:

Look at the graph on the crab. Answer the questions.

⑤　Who caught the most fish?　_____

⑥　How many fish did the crabs catch altogether?　_____ fish

1   Numbers to 100 (1)

1. 68 ; 8 ; 60 ; 8   2. 47 ; 4 ; 7 ; 40 ; 7
3. 35 ; 3 ; 5 ; 30 ; 5
4. 42   5. 84   6. 51
7. 26   8. 70 ; 3   9. 90 ; 7
10. 47 ; 48 ; 50 ; 51 ; 54 ; 55 ; 56 ; 59 ; 61 ; 62 ; 64 ; 65 ; 67 ; 68 ;
    70 ; 71 ; 74 ; 75 ; 76
11. 91 ; 89 ; 88 ; 85 ; 84 ; 83 ; 80 ; 79 ; 77 ; 76 ; 74 ; 73 ; 69 ; 68 ;
    67 ; 65 ; 63 ; 62
12. 13. 14.

2   Numbers to 100 (2)

1. 39   2. 64   3. 53
4. 36
5. 40, 39, 36 ;
6. 98, 90, 88, 83 ;
7. 72, 66, 53, 45 ;
8. 54, 33, 28, 19 ;
9. 25   10. 49   11. 36
12. 54   13. 71   14. 82
15. 67   16. 94   17. 38
18. 63   19. 43   20. 76
21. Forty-six   22. Fifty-nine   23. Eighty-three
24. Ninety-four 25. Sixty-two   26. Thirty-seven
27. Seventy-five 28. Twenty-one
29A: 30   B: 74   C: 29
    D: 95   E: 25   F: 50

3   Ordinal Numbers

1. 25   2. 76th   3. 51st
4. 33rd   5. 84th   6. 98th
7. fortieth   8. sixty-nineth   9. seventy-third
10. eightieth   11. forty-second 12. ninety-first
13.

14a. 38th ; 39th ; 41st   b. 5
   c. The 43rd   d. The 39th
15. 54th ; 27th ; 10th   16. 75th

4   Addition of 2-Digit Numbers

1. 49   2. 64   3. 66
4. 91   5. 45   6. 67
7. 87   8. 39   9. 74
10. 73   11. 71   12. 64
13. 93
14. Colour the balls with these numbers:
    73, 41, 38, 85, 42, 92, 72, 81, 49, 46, 60, 80
15a. 36 + 48 ; 84 ; 84   b. 48 + 48 ; 96 ; 96
   c. 36 + 36 ; 72 ; 72
16a. 15 + 26 ; 41 ; 41   b. 24 + 17 ; 41 ; 41
   c. 15 + 24 ; 39 ; 39   d. 26 + 17 ; 43 ; 43
   e. 39 + 43 ; 82 ; 82

5   Subtraction of 2-Digit Numbers

1. 8   2. 28   3. 19
4. 14   5. 58   6. 26
7. 19   8. 59   9. 17
10. 8   11. 39   12. 13
13. 19 ; 39   14. 26 ; 36   15. 81 ; 71
16. 65 ; 45   17. $\begin{array}{r} 82 \\ -17 \\ \hline 65 \end{array}$; 65   18. $\begin{array}{r} 75 \\ -45 \\ \hline 30 \end{array}$; 30
19. $\begin{array}{r} 53 \\ -45 \\ \hline 8 \end{array}$; 8   20. $\begin{array}{r} 80 \\ -75 \\ \hline 5 \end{array}$; 5   21. $\begin{array}{r} 80 \\ -9 \\ \hline 71 \end{array}$; 71

6   Addition and Subtraction of 2-Digit Numbers

1. 13   2. 91   3. 81
4. 68   5. 64   6. 48
7. 75   8. 45   9. 58
10. 32   11. 22   12. 92
13. 71   14. 57   15. 16
16. 51   17. 10   18. 53
19. B, D, E, F
20a. $\begin{array}{r} 56 \\ +37 \\ \hline 93 \end{array}$; 93   b. $\begin{array}{r} 56 \\ -37 \\ \hline 19 \end{array}$; 19
21a. $\begin{array}{r} 64 \\ -35 \\ \hline 29 \end{array}$; 29   b. $\begin{array}{r} 64 \\ +35 \\ \hline 99 \end{array}$; 99   22. $\begin{array}{r} 18 \\ +35 \\ \hline 53 \end{array}$; 53

7   Numbers to 1000

1. 3 ; 6 ; 7 ; 367   2. 4 ; 2 ; 5 ; 425   3. 2 ; 3 ; 9 ; 239
4. 300 ; 90 ; 8   5. 500 ; 70 ; 2   6. 800 ; 60 ; 3
7. 330 ; 331 ; 333   8. 851 ; 853 ; 854   9. 797 ; 798 ; 800
10. 470 ; 471 ; 474
11. 600   12. 459   13. 7
14. (Suggested answers) 621 ; 650
15A. 306   B. 419   C. 300
   1. 374   2. 930   3. 400

8   Counting by 10's or 25's

1. 470 ; 480 ; 490 ; 500 ; 520 ; 540 ; 560 ; 570 ; 580 ; 600
2. 75 ; 100 ; 150 ; 200 ; 225 ; 300 ; 325 ; 350 ; 425 ; 450
3. 890 ; 900 ; 910 ; 930 ; 940 ; 950 ; 970
4. 740 ; 730 ; 720 ; 700 ; 690 ; 670 ; 640 ; 630 ; 610 ; 600 ; 590
5.
6.
7.   ; By 25's

9   Counting by 50's or 100's

1. 600 ; 650   2. 400 ; 500 ; 600   3. 250 ; 300 ; 400
4. 600 ; 700 ; 900   5. 750 ; 800 ; 900
6. 50 ; 100 ; 150 ; 200 ; 250 ; 300 ; 350 ; 400 ; 450 ; 500
7. 100 ; 200 ; 300 ; 400 ; 500

8.

— girl's path
— boy's path

9. 100 ; 200 ; 300 ; 400 ; 500 ; 600 ; 700 ; 800
10. 50 ; 100 ; 150 ; 200 ; 250 ; 300 ; 350 ; 400 ; 450 ; 500 ; 550 ;
    600 ; 650 ; 700 ; 750 ; 800
11. 8   12. 16   13. Lily
14. No

10 Addition of 3-Digit Numbers (1)

1. 437   2. 747   3. 597
4. 477   5. 854   6. 289
7. 279   8. 387   9. 688
10. 527   11. 377   12. 638
13. 668   14. 683   15. 499
10-15. (Colour the box in 14.)
16. 415 + 74 ; 489 ; 489   17. 130 + 130 ; 260 ; 260
18. 245 + 42 ; 287 ; 287   19. 327 + 60 ; 387 ; 387
20a.   14 ; 148   b.   148 ; 178
     + 134   + 30
      148   178

11 Addition of 3-Digit Numbers (2)

1A: 480 ; ✔   B: 473   C: 413
2A: 842   B: 751   C: 901 ; ✔
3A: 374   B: 421   C: 439 ; ✔
4A: 925   B: 981 ; ✔   C: 921
5.   427 ; 792   6.   108 ; 164   7.   137 ; 231
   + 365   + 56   + 94
    792   164   231
8a.   73 ; 361   b.   361 ; 427
    + 288   + 66
     361   427

12 Subtraction of 3-Digit Numbers (1)

1. 219   2. 313   3. 612
4. 815   5. 192   6. 326
7. 79   8. 151   9. 325
10. 505   11. watermelon
12. 659 – 523 ; 136 ; 136   13. 865 – 659 ; 206 ; 206
14. 523 – 463 ; 60 ; 60   15. 659 – 338 ; 321 ; 321
16. 865 – 463 ; 402 ; 402
17. Strawberry juice was the most popular because it was a
    special.

13 Subtraction of 3-Digit Numbers (2)

1. 189   2. 585   3. 384
4. 135   5. 298   6. 278
7. 156: match with the fourth box (621 – 465 = 156)
   367: match with the second box (416 – 49 = 367)
   419: match with the third box (705 – 286 = 419)
   399: match with the first box (828 – 429 = 399)
8.   729 ; 302   9.   400 ; 235
   – 427   – 165
    302   235
10.   108 ; 69   11.   322 ; 163
    – 39   – 159
      69   163

14 Addition and Subtraction of 3-Digit Numbers

1. 486   2. 690   3. 226
4. 223   5. 442   6. 693
7. 116   8. 266   9. 563
10. 692
11.

168   157   549   559
      147   219
270   557
      557   587
            567   471
118
      128   660   481
              191   588
            560   171
                    181
12. 174 + 49 ; 223 ; 223   13. 752 – 298 ; 454 ; 454
14. 287 + 325 ; 612 ; 612
15a. 109 + 82 ; 191 ; 191   b. 109 – 82 ; 27 ; 27

15 Estimating Sums and Differences

1. 900   2. 600   3. 300
4. 900   5. 600   6. 500
7. 100   8. 600   9. 200
10. 400   11. 600   12. 700
13.   400 ; 626   14.   500 ; 960
    + 300   + 400
      700   900
15.   800 ; 368   16.   700 ; 591
    – 500   – 100
      300   600
17. (Calculate and colour A, B, E, H, L, and M.)
17A. 720   B. 737   E. 728
H. 528   L. 649   M. 902
18. 600 ; 500

16 Relating Addition and Subtraction

1. 169   2. 514   3. 500
4. 925
5-8. (Suggested answers)
5. 146, 381 ; 527   6. 427, 498 ; 925
   527, 146 ; 381   925, 427 ; 498
7. 271, 356 ; 627   8. 46, 362 ; 408
   627, 271 ; 356   408, 46 ; 362
9A: 327   B: 294   C: 693
D: 832   E: 417   F: 551
G: 677
   294 + 138 = 432 ; B   693 – 566 = 127 ; C
   273 + 327 = 600 ; A   417 + 154 = 571 ; E
   832 – 479 = 353 ; D   677 – 293 = 384 ; G
   551 + 189 = 740 ; F
10. 653   11. 427

17 Review

1. 85 ; 86 ; 87 ; 89 ; 90 ; 91   2. 928 ; 929 ; 930 ; 931
3. 560 ; 561 ; 562 ; 564   4. 50 ; 75 ; 100 ; 125 ; 150 ; 175
5. 400 ; 500 ; 600 ; 700 ; 800 ; 900
6. 700 ; 750 ; 800 ; 850 ; 900 ; 950
7. 58   8. 91   9. 594
10. 37   11. 155   12. 441
13. 335   14. 256   15. 855
16. 189   17. 168   18. 808
19. 89   20. 905   21. 600
22. 81st   23. 39th
24.   800 ;   827 ; 498   25.   500 ;   492 ; 860
    – 300   – 329   + 400   + 368
      500   498   900   860

26.
```
  400  ;   406   ; 249
- 200    - 157
  200      249
```

18 You Deserve A Break!

1. Ten ; Twenty-five ; Fifty
2.

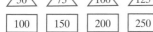

3. 50 ; 125 ; 250
4. 203   5. 40   6. 56th
7. 55th   8. 57th   9. 836
10. 224   11. 95   12. 674

19 Checking Subtraction by Using Addition

1. 573 ; ✔   2.
```
  289 ; ✗
+ 666
  955
```
3. 582 ; ✗

4. 338 ; 489 ; 827 ; ✔   5. 149 ; 151 ; 300 ; ✗
6. 88 ; 512 ; 600 ; ✔   7. 169 ; 237 ; 406 ; ✔
8.
```
  273  ;  159  ; 159
- 114    + 114
  159      273
```
9.
```
  287  ;  139  ; 139
- 148    + 148
  139      287
```
10.
```
  312  ;   93  ; 93
- 219    + 219
   93      312
```
11.
```
  680  ;  149  ; 149
- 531    + 531
  149      680
```

20 Length and Distance (1)

1.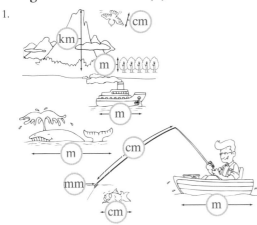
2.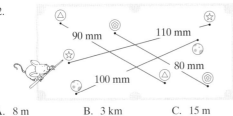

3A. 8 m   B. 3 km   C. 15 m
D. 350 m   E. 3 m   F. 85 m

21 Length and Distance (2)

1. 2000   2. 3   3. 60
4. 400   5. 7000   6. 2
7. 70   8. 45   9. 3000
10. 5600   11. 28   12. 716
13. 524 cm   14. 15 km   15. 22 cm

16.

17. 26 mm   18. 2 cm   19. 4040
20. A to C, then to E ; 1 km   21. 3

22 Days and Years

1.

2. normal   3. July 1 ; October 31 ; December 25
4. January 1 ; December 31
5.   6. 366

7. 2004   8. 2012   9. 14 ; Thursday
10. January 14   11. 12   12. 7

23 Weeks and Years

1. January 8 ; January 14   2. March 7
3. 4   4. on or before March 22
5. 14   6. May 11
7. July 15 8. 18
9. June 13 ; July 23 ; 5 ; 5   10. 5
11. 3   12. 4
13. 4

24 Telling Time

1. 5 minutes past 12   2. 25 minutes to 11
3. 03 ; 40 ; 20 minutes to 4
4. 09 ; 25 ; 25 minutes past 9
5. 11 ; 10 ; 10 minutes past 11
6. 02 ; 55 ; 5 minutes to 3
7A. 10 ; 08 ;   B. 2 ; 33 ;   C. 7 ; 19 ;
8. May 10   9. 2 ; 28   10. 8 ; 00

25 Passage of Time

1.   2. 05 ; 53 ; 08 ; 21
3. 20 ; 25 ; 45 ; 55 4. 45   5. 11:08
6. 5:47   7. 40   8. 1 ; 10

26 Temperatures

1A. 35 ; Raium   B. 60 ; Combex   C. 70 ; Sydex
D. 15 ; Katium
2. Sydex   3. 25°C
4A. 98°C   B. 10°C   C. 2°C
D. 15°C   E. 70°C
5. decrease ; 8°C 6. will not ; 52°C 7. Summer

27 Perimeter

1A. 16 cm   B. 24 cm   C. 30 m
D. 16 m   E. 14 cm   F. 20 cm
G. 43 cm   H. 18 m
2. (Suggested answer)

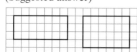

3. Perimeter: 24 ; 16 ; 24 ; 16 ; 80
   Length: 80 ; 35 ; 10 ; 35
4. Length: 20 ÷ 2 ; 10
   Perimeter: 7 + 10 + 7 + 10 ; 34

28 Area

1A. 8   B. 12   C. 13
D. 14   E. 12   F. 10
2. D   3. A
4-7. (Suggested drawings)

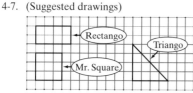

8. square ; yes   9. 4

29 Money (1)

1.

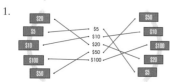

2. Check any 2 $20 bills and 1 $10 bill.
3. Check any 5 $20 bills.
4. $430 ; $395 ; $380
5. Mr. Wolf   6. Uncle Peter   7. $15
8A. $269   B. $218

30 Money (2)

1A. 1 dollar 32 cents ; 1.32
B. 5 dollars 17 cents ; 5.17
C. 20 dollars 77 cents ; 20.77
D. 100 dollars 16 cents ; 100.16
E. 67 dollars 46 cents ; 67.46
2.

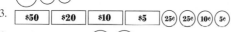

8. (Suggested answer)

1st way	2nd way

31 Addition and Subtraction with Money

1.
```
  5 55  ;   5 55
+ 4 19    - 4 19
  9 74      1 36
```
2.
```
  6 43  ;   6 43
+ 2 88    - 2 88
  9 31      3 55
```
3. $9.16   4. $4.41   5. $5.75
6. $5.82
7a.
```
  7 59  ; 9.77
+ 2 18
  9 77
```
 b.
```
  7 59  ; 5.41
- 2 18
  5 41
```
8a.
```
  5 29  ; 10.58
+ 5 29
 10 58
```
 b.
```
  5 29  ; 4.84
-   45
  4 84
```
9a.
```
  2 75  ; 2.57
-   18
  2 57
```
 b.
```
  2 75  ; 5.32
+ 2 57
  5 32
```
 c.
```
  2 75  ; 5.50
+ 2 75
  5 50
```

32 Capacity (1)

1. 10 L   2. 100 L   3. 1 L
4. 2 L   5. 25 L   6. 1 L
7. 75 L
8a. 80 L   b. 50 L   c. 1 L
d. 12 L
9. 1 L   10. 36 oranges 11. 3 jugs
12. 180 L

33 Capacity (2)

1A. 425 mL   B. 212 mL   C. 500 mL
D. 825 mL   E. 972 mL   F. 288 mL
2. E   3. B   4. A, B, and F
5. 850 mL   6. 760 mL   7. B and F
8. 750 mL   9. 120 mL   10. 20 mL
11. 35 mL   12. 280 mL 13. 310 mL
14a. 880 mL b. 950 mL c. 820 mL
d. 1 L

34 Mass (1)

1. 2 kg   2. 1 kg   3. 8 kg
4. 500 kg
5A. 4 kg   B. 5 kg   C. 10 kg
D. 2 kg   E. 3 kg   F. 1 kg
6. 30 kg   7. 25 kg   8. 75 kg
9. 60 kg   10. 6   11. 5
12. 17   13. 15
14. Eva: gain ; 2
    Martin: gain ; 3
    Mr. Smith: lose ; 1
    Mrs. Smith: gain ; 1

35 Review

1. 45 ;   ;   2. 35 ; 9 ; 50 ; 25 ; past 10

3. 15 min   4. 10

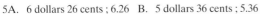
5A. 6 dollars 26 cents ; 6.26   B.   5 dollars 36 cents ; 5.36

6.
```
    6  26    ;    6  26
  + 5  36       - 5  36
  ---------    ---------
   11  62          90
```

7. 238 + 189 = 427 ; ✔   8.   189 + 416 = 605 ; ✔
9. 173 + 128 = 301 ; ✗   10.   306 + 216 = 522 ; ✗
11. $5.14   12. $7.25   13. $4.18
14. $2.66   15. $0.35   16. $7.52
17A. 14 ; 11   B.   15 ; 13
18. 95 ; 3   19. 10 ; 500

36   You Deserve A Break!

1. A ; 5 ; 29 ; C ; 4 ; 35 ; D ; 3 ; 50 ; B ; 2 ; 49
2. 1 km   3. 40 mm   4. 68 cm
5. 24 cm   6. 5 m
7.
   2 L •————————• has the greatest capacity

   4 L •————————• holds 2 times a litre

   385 mL •————————• has the smallest capacity

   982 mL •————————• holds almost a litre
8. 15 ; 08 ; 28 ; 08   9.   Nov 29, 2008 ; Dec 12, 2008

37   Mass (2)

1.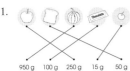

   950 g   100 g   250 g   15 g   50 g

2. 140 g   3. 420 g   4. 950 g
5. 85 g   6. 820 g   7. 90 g
8. 125 g   9. 275 g
10A. 600 g   B. 450 g   C. 550 g
D. 400 g   E. 530 g
11. A, C, and E   12. A, C, and E   13. 3
14.
15.

38   Multiplying by 2, 5, or 0

1a. 6   b. 16   c. 10
d. 12   e. 4   f. 2
g. 18   h. 8   i. 14
j. 20
2a. 0   b. 0   c. 0
d. 0   e. 0   f. 0
3a. 25   b. 35   c. 20
d. 10   e. 5   f. 15
g. 45   h. 40   i. 30
j. 50
4. 6 ; 5 ; 30 ; 30   5. 9 ; 5 ; 45 ; 45
6. 8 ; 2 ; 16 ; 16   7. 7 ; 2 ; 14 ; 14
8. 5 ; 2 ; 10 ; 10
9a. 3 ; 0 ; 0 ; 0   b. 9 ; 0 ; 0 ; 0

39   Multiplying by 1, 3, or 4

1a. 24   b. 18   c. 12
d. 15   e. 6   f. 21
g. 27

2a. 9   b. 7   c. 6
d. 5   e. 2   f. 8
g. 3
3a. 36   b. 20   c. 12
d. 24   e. 28   f. 8
g. 4
4.
```
    3  ; 21
  x 7
  ------
   21
```
5.
```
    4  ; 24
  x 6
  ------
   24
```
6.
```
    1  ; 5
  x 5
  ------
    5
```
7.
```
    3  ; 9
  x 3
  -----
    9
```
8.
```
    3  ; 27
  x 9
  ------
   27
```

40   Multiplying by 6 or 7

1.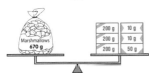

a. 30   b. 18   c. 42
d. 6   e. 54   f. 24
g. 12   h. 36   i. 60
2.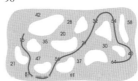

a. 14   b. 42   c. 28
d. 21   e. 63   f. 7
g. 35   h. 56   i. 49
3. 5 x 6 ; 30 ; 30   4. 3 x 7 ; 21 ; 21
5. 4 x 6 ; 24 ; 24   6. 9 x 6 ; 54 ; 54
7. 3 x 6 ; 18 ; 18   8. 5 x 7 ; 35 ; 35

41   Multiplying by 8 or 9

1. 24   2. 18   3. 45
4. 16   5. 56   6. 27
7. 81   8. 54   9. 32
10. 72   11. 36   12. 48
13. 90
14.

15. No. of Chocolates in all: 32 ; 40 ; 48 ; 56
    Cost($): 36 ; 45 ; 54 ; 63
16. No. of Muffins in all: 27 ; 54 ; 72 ; 81
    Cost($): 24 ; 48 ; 64 ; 72
17. 3 x 9 ; 27 ; 27   18. 2 x 9 ; 18 ; 18
19. 8 x 8 ; 64 ; 64
20. 2 x 9 ; 18 ; 18 + 8 ; 26 ; 26

42   Solving Problems Involving Multiplication

1a. 30   b. 45
2a. 9   b. 24
3a. 12   b. 42
4a. 8   b. 40
5.
```
    9  ; 36
  x 4
  ------
   36
```
6.
```
    3  ; 9
  x 3
  -----
    9
```
7.
```
    4  ; 28
  x 7
  ------
   28
```
8.
```
    8  ; 72
  x 9
  ------
   72
```
9.
```
    6  ; 30
  x 5
  ------
   30
```

43 More about Multiplication

1. ; 5
2. ; 3
3. ; 4
4. 24 ; 24   5. 42 ; 42   6. 20 ; 20
7. 18 ; 18   8. 18 ; 18   9. 56 ; 56
10. 63 ; 63   11. 40 ; 40   12. 12 ; 12
13. product   14. 6   15. 9

44 Introducing Division

1a. ; 15   b. 3
2a. ; 24   b. 4
3a. ; 4   b. 2
4. ; 16 ; 4
5. ; 10 ; 5
6. ; 20 ; 4
7. ; 6 ; 2

45 Dividing by 1, 2, or 3

1. 4 ; $\frac{4}{2\overline{)8}}$ 2. 4 ; $\frac{4}{3\overline{)12}}$

3. 5 ; $\frac{5}{1\overline{)5}}$ 4. 5 ; $\frac{5}{2\overline{)10}}$

5a. 9   b. 3
c. 7   d. 6
6a. 6   b. 3
c. 7   d. 5
7. $\frac{4}{3\overline{)12}}$ 8. $\frac{7}{2\overline{)14}}$ 9. $\frac{8}{3\overline{)24}}$
10. $\frac{8}{1\overline{)8}}$ 11. 5   12. 5
13. 9   14. 9   15. 2
16. 9   17. 6   18. 7
19. 3   20. 12 ÷ 3 ; 4 ; 4
21. 18 ÷ 2 ; 9 ; 9   22. 16 ÷ 2 ; 8 ; 8

46 Dividing by 4 or 5

1a. $\frac{6}{4\overline{)24}}$ b. $\frac{4}{4\overline{)16}}$
c. 5   d. 2
e. 1   f. 3

2a. $\frac{7}{5\overline{)35}}$ b. $\frac{5}{5\overline{)25}}$
c. 4   d. 8   e. 3
f. 1   g. 2   h. 9
i. 6   j. 10
3. 35 ÷ 5 ; 7 ; 7   4. 12 ÷ 4 ; 3 ; 3
5. 24 ÷ 4 ; 6 ; 6
6a. 20 ÷ 4 ; 5 ; 5   b. 20 ÷ 5 ; 4 ; 4

47 Dividing by 6 or 7

1a.
b. 1   c. 2   d. 3
e. 4   f. 5   g. 6
h. 7   i. 8   j. 9
2a.
b. 1   c. 2   d. 3
e. 4   f. 5   g. 6
h. 7   i. 8   j. 9
3. $\frac{4}{6\overline{)24}}$; 4   4. $\frac{8}{7\overline{)56}}$; 8   5. $\frac{8}{6\overline{)48}}$; 8
6. $\frac{6}{6\overline{)36}}$; 6   7. $\frac{9}{7\overline{)63}}$; 9

48 Dividing by 8 or 9

1. $\frac{4}{9\overline{)36}}$ 2. $\frac{5}{8\overline{)40}}$ 3. $\frac{9}{9\overline{)81}}$
4. 2   5. 7   6. 7
7. 6   8. 1   9. 8
10A. 8   B. 2   C. 5
D. 3   E. 4   F. 9
G. 1
11a. 56 ÷ 8 ; 7 ; 7   b. 32 ÷ 8 ; 4 ; 4
12a. 72 ÷ 9 ; 8 ; 8   b. 27 ÷ 9 ; 3 ; 3
13a. 16 ÷ 8 ; 2 ; 2   b. 64 ÷ 8 ; 8 ; 8
14. 45 ÷ 9 ; 5 ; 5

49 Solving Problems Involving Division

1A. 3   B. 5   C. 3
D. 3   E. 4   F. 7
G. 7   H. 8   I. 6
J. 5
2. 3   3. 9   4. 8
5. 7
6a. 24 ÷ 3 = 8 ; 24 ÷ 6 = 4 ; 24 ÷ 8 = 3
b. 36 ÷ 4 = 9 ; 36 ÷ 6 = 6 ; 36 ÷ 9 = 4
7. $\frac{6}{4\overline{)24}}$; 6   8. $\frac{6}{6\overline{)36}}$; 6   9. $\frac{3}{3\overline{)9}}$; 3

50 More about Division

1. Circle every 3 pictures. ; 4
   Circle every 4 pictures. ; 3
2. Circle every 2 pictures. ; 5
   Circle every 5 pictures. ; 2
3. Circle every 3 pictures. ; 5
   Circle every 5 pictures. ; 3

4. 8   5. 16   6. 5
7. 56   8. 9   9. 35
10. 9 ; 5   11. 7 ; 9   12. 5 ; 7
13. 4 ; 9

51 Division with Remainders (1)

1.  ; 4R1

2.  ; 4R3

3.
```
    5R5
  6)35
    30
     5
```
4.
```
    5R1
  4)21
    20
     1
```
5.
```
    5R5
  8)45
    40
     5
```
6.
```
    2R4
  7)18
    14
     4
```
7. 5R5   8. 7R1

9. 3R1   10. 5R4   11. 45 ÷ 6 ; 7R3 ; 7 ; 3
12. 23 ÷ 5 ; 4R3 ; 4 ; 3   13. 42 ÷ 8 ; 5R2 ; 5 ; 2
14. 75 ÷ 9 ; 8R3 ; 8 ; 3

52 Division with Remainders (2)

1.
```
    9R1
  8)73
    72
     1
```
2.
```
    8R2
  5)42
    40
     2
```
3.
```
    7R5
  9)68
    63
     5
```
4.
```
    4R1
  7)29
    28
     1
```
5. 9R1   6. 8R4

7. 6R4   8. 2R5   9. 8R2
10. 6R4
11.  ; 3R2 ; 4

12.  ; 8R1 ; 9

13.
```
    6R4
  5)34
    30
     4
```
14.
```
    8R2
  6)50
    48
     2
```
15.
```
    7R3
  4)31
    28
     3
```
16. 45 ÷ 6 ; 7R3 ; 8   17. 17 ÷ 4 ; 4R1 ; 5
18. 29 ÷ 3 ; 9R2 ; 10   19. 24 ÷ 9 ; 2R6 ; 3

53 Review

1a. 40   b. 8
2a. 30   b. 5
3a. 21   b. 7
4. 27   5. 24   6. 45
7. 56
8.
```
     9
  6)54
    54
```
9.
```
    4R2
  8)34
    32
     2
```
10.
```
     9
  2)18
    18
```
11.
```
    9R1
  9)82
    81
     1
```
12. 28   13. 18

14. 3R1   15. 8R1   16. 20

17. 12   18. 1R6   19. 49
20. 7
21a. 350 g   b. 450 g
  c. 160 g   d. 550 g
22. 16 ÷ 2 ; 8 ; 8   23. 7 x 2 ; 14 ; 14
24. 9 x 3 ; 27 ; 27   25. 40 ÷ 6 ; 6R4 ; 7

54 You Deserve A Break!

1. 2: 2 ; 4 ; 6 ; 8 ; 10 ; 12 ; 14 ; 16 ; 18
   5: 5 ; 10 ; 15 ; 20 ; 25 ; 30 ; 35 ; 40 ; 45
2.
```
    9R3
  4)39
    36
     3
```
3.
```
    7R4
  5)39
    35
     4
```
4.
```
    6R3
  6)39
    36
     3
```
5.
```
    5R4
  7)39
    35
     4
```
6. 4R7   7. 4R3

8a. 12   b. 4
9a. 35   b. 7
10. 16   11. 4   12. 8

55 Divisibility of 2, 5, or 10

1. 6 ; 28 ; 10 ; 18 ; 24 ; 52 ; 86
2.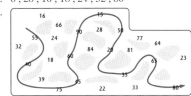

3A.
```
     5
 10)50
    50
```
C.
```
     4
 10)40
    40
```
E. 3   I. 6   J. 8
4. 10 ; 40 ; 90 ; 20   5. 30 ; 70 ; 50 ; 80
6. 362, 364, 366, and 368   7. 425, 430, 435, and 440
8. 850, 860, and 870

56 Two-step Problems

1. 14 ; 58 ; 72 ; 72 ; 9 ; 8   2. 60 – 4 ; 56 ; 56 ÷ 7 ; 8
3. 4 + 5 ; 9 ; 7 x 9 ; 63
4. Number of pizzas: 4 x 4 = 16 ;
   Number of plates needed: 16 ÷ 2 = 8 ; 8
5. Total number of slices: 4 x 8 = 32 ;
   Number of slices left: 32 – 25 = 7 ; 7
6. Number of candies left: 65 – 9 = 56 ;
   Number of candies for each girl: 56 ÷ 8 = 7 ; 7
7. Total amount of money: 4 x $5 = $20 ;
   Amount of money left: $20 – $3 = $17 ; 17

57 Relating Multiplication and Division

1. 30 ; 5 ; 6 ; 6   2. 56 ; 7 ; 8 ; 56
3. 9 ; 27 ; 3 ; 9 ; 3 ; 27 ; 9   4. 6 ; 24 ; 4 ; 24 ; 4 ; 6 ; 24 ; 6
5-8. (Suggested answers)
5. 6 ; 9 ; 54 ; 54 ; 6 ; 9   6. 5 ; 7 ; 35 ; 35 ; 5 ; 7
7. 2 ; 8 ; 16 ; 16 ; 2 ; 8   8. 4 ; 9 ; 36 ; 36 ; 4 ; 9
9. 8   10. 9   11. 115
12. 24   13.   14.

58 Fractions (1)

1. ; $\frac{2}{8}$ 2. ; $\frac{3}{5}$ 3. ; $\frac{2}{6}$

4.  ; $\frac{2}{7}$

5. 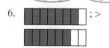 ; $\frac{3}{4}$

6. ; >

7. ; >

8. ; >

9. ; <

10. 4   11. $\frac{2}{4}$ 12. $\frac{1}{4}$

13. 8   14. $\frac{4}{8}$ 15. $\frac{3}{8}$

59   Fractions (2)

1. $3\frac{4}{6}$ 2. $2\frac{7}{10}$ 3. $4\frac{5}{12}$

4. $6\frac{3}{7}$ 5. 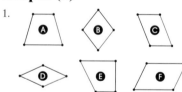   6.

7. 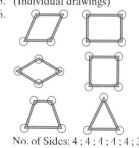   8. $3\frac{3}{4}$ 9. $2\frac{3}{5}$

10. $4\frac{2}{7}$ 11. $3\frac{7}{9}$ 12. $7\frac{1}{10}$

13. $5\frac{1}{4}$ 14. $2\frac{3}{8}$ 15. $6\frac{1}{6}$

16. $\frac{6}{8}$; $1\frac{2}{8}$ 17. $1\frac{7}{10}$; $2\frac{3}{10}$

60   Shapes (1)

1.

Parallelogram: C, F ; Rhombus: B, D ; Trapezoid: A, E

2. 8 ; 3 ; 3 ; 2

3-5. (Individual drawings)

6.

No. of Sides: 4 ; 4 ; 4 ; 4 ; 4 ; 3

No. of Vertices: 4 ; 4 ; 4 ; 4 ; 4 ; 3

61   Shapes (2)

1. C   2. A ; D   3. B

4. 1 ; 4   5. 1 square ; 4 trapezoids

6. 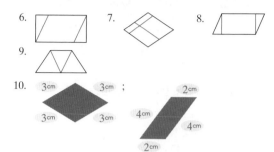   7.   8.

9.

10. ;

11. ✔   12.   13. ✔

62   Congruent and Similar Shapes

1A. similar   B. congruent   C. congruent

D. similar   E. congruent   F. similar

2.   3.

4.   5.

6. congruent   7. similar   8. similar

9.   10.

63   Tile Patterns

1-8. Colour 1, 2, 4, 6, and 8.

1. Trapezoid   2. Rhombus   4. Triangle

6. Parallelogram   8. Hexagon

9.   10.

11.   12.

13. (Suggested answers)

64   Lines of Symmetry

1.   3.   4.

5.   6.

8A. ; 3   B. ; 6   C. ; 2

9.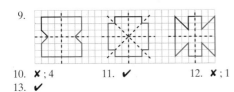

10. ✘ ; 4   11. ✔   12. ✘ ; 1
13. ✔

65 Naming 3-D Figures

1.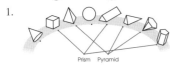

   Prism   Pyramid

2. Triangle ; Triangular prism
3. Hexagon ; Hexagonal prism
4. Pentagon ; Pentagonal prism
5A. Hexagon ; Hexagonal pyramid
 B. Triangle ; Triangular pyramid
 C. Square ; Square-based pyramid
 D. Pentagon ; Pentagonal pyramid
6. Rectangular pyramid   7. Triangular prism
8. Hexagonal prism   9. Pentagonal pyramid

66 Sorting 3-D Figures

1. A, C, D, F ; B, E   2. A, B, C, E ; D, F
3. A, C, F ; B, D, E   4. A, C, F ; B, D, E
5. A, C, F ; B, D, E   6. B
7. A   8. C   9. B ; C
10. A ; D   11. B ; D

67 Constructing 3-D Figures

1A. Rectangular prism   B. Triangular prism
 C. Hexagonal prism   D. Rectangular pyramid
 E. Triangular pyramid
2. ; rectangular prism ; 8 ; 12

3. ; hexagonal pyramid ; 7 ; 12

4.   5.

6.   7.

8. triangular   9. 12 ; 7
10. 5 ; pentagonal pyramid

68 Nets of 3-D Figures

1. 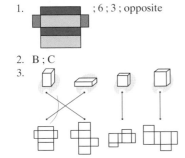 ; 6 ; 3 ; opposite

2. B ; C
3.

4.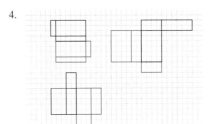

69 Transformations – Translation

1. A ; C ; F ; G   2.   3.
4.   5.

6.   7.

8. Colour A, B, and E.

70 Transformations – Reflection

1. A ; D   2.   3.
4.   5.

6.   7.

8.

71 Review

1. Divisible by 2: 56 ; 42 ; 34 ; 10 ; 18
   Divisible by 5: 50 ; 20 ; 15 ; 85
   Divisible by 2 and 10: 40 ; 60 ; 90 ; 80
2. 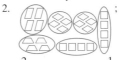 ;

   a. $\frac{2}{6}$ b. $\frac{1}{6}$ c. $\frac{2}{6}$

3.  ;

   a. $2\frac{1}{4}$ b. $1\frac{3}{4}$
4. $\frac{5}{9}$ 5. $\frac{6}{7}$ 6. $2\frac{1}{5}$
7. $4\frac{5}{8}$

8A. Rectangular pyramid B. Rectangular prism
C. Pentagonal pyramid D. Triangular prism
9. C ; D   10. A ; C ; D   11. B
12. 13.
14. 16 – 2 ; 14 ; 14 ÷ 2 ; 7   15. 17

72 You Deserve A Break!

1.
2.
3a. Rectangular pyramid ; 5 ; 8
b. Rectangular prism ; 8 ; 12
c. Triangular prism ; 6 ; 9
4. $\frac{4}{8}$; $\frac{3}{8}$; $\frac{1}{8}$
5a. 46 ; 62 ; 18   b. 40 ; 60 ; 30
6. 24 ÷ 4 = 6 ; 6 x 2 = 12 ; 12

73 Transformations – Rotation (1)

1-7. Colour 2, 3, 6, and 7.
8.   9.   10.
11.   12.   13.
14.
A quarter turn
A half turn
A three-quarter turn
15.
A quarter turn
A half turn
A three-quarter turn

74 Transformations – Rotation (2)

1.   2.   3.
4.   5.   6.
7. ; $\frac{1}{2}$ 8. ; $\frac{1}{4}$
9. ; $\frac{3}{4}$ 10 ; quarter
11. ; half   12. ; three-quarter

13. ; half   14. Yes

75 More about Transformations

1. Reflection   2. Translation   3. Rotation
4. Translation   5. Rotation   6. Reflection
7-8 (Suggested answers)
7.
8.
9B. Rotation   C. Reflection   E. Translation
10A. Rotation   C. Reflection   D. Translation
11. (Suggested answers)
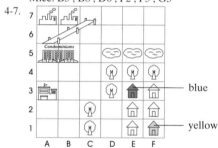

76 Coordinates (1)

1. 7 ; A ; G   2. 8 ; 1 ; 8
3. Cats: A4 ; C1 ; C7 ; E3 ; E8 ; G7
Mice: B5 ; B8 ; D6 ; F2 ; F5 ; G3
4-7.
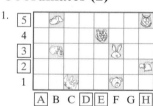
blue
yellow
A B C D E F
8. A5 and B5   9. (Suggested answer) A5

77 Coordinates (2)

1.

2. Elephant ; B3   3. Rabbit ; F3   4. Tiger ; E4
5-6.
7. 1 ; left ; 1 ; up   8. 2 ; C1 and C2   9. 2 ; B5 and A3
10. Yes

78 Identifying Patterns

1. pattern ; size   2. orientation ; shape
3. colour ; position   4. orientation ; size
5. pattern ; position

6a.   b. square ; square ; square

c. small ; small

7a.   b. left ; left ; right ; left

c. dots ; stripes ; stripes

8a.   b. outside ; inside

c. grey ; grey ; white

79 Creating Patterns

1. ♡○♡○♡○♡○♡○♡○♡ ; colour ; size

B Y G B Y G B Y G B Y G

B = blue, Y = yellow, G = green

2. □   □   □   □ ; position ; orientation
♡ ♡ ♡ ♡ ♡ ♡ ♡ ♡ ♡
□ □   □ □   □ □

3. ⊘⊘⊘⊘⊘⊘⊘⊘⊘ ; pattern ; orientation

4-5. (Suggested answers)

4. △○ ○ △ ○ △ ○ △ ○ ○ ○

5.

6.

7.

8.   9.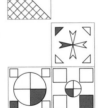

80 Number Patterns

1. 20 ; 24 ; 32 ; 36   2. 80 ; 70 ; 65 ; 50
3. 70 ; 62 ; 57 ; 52   4. 5 ; 9 ; 18 ; 17
5. 87 ; 91 ; 88   6. 60 ; 50 ; 52
7. 41 ; 47 ; 52
8A. 60   B. 30
  C. 30   D. 15
9A. 11   B. 10
  C. 25   D. 10
10a. 5 ; 9 ; 13 ; 17 ; 21   b. 65
11a. 3 ; 6 ; 9 ; 12 ; 15   b. 18

81 Patterns in a Hundreds Chart

1. 7 ; 14 ; 21 ; 28 ; 35 ; 42 ; 49 ; 56 ; 63 ; 70 ; Colour these numbers in the chart red.
2. Colour 77, 84, 91, and 98 yellow.
3a. 77   b. 84   c. 91
  d. 98
4a. Colour: 31 ; 32 ; 33 ; 34 ; 35 ; 22 ; 23 ; 24 ; 25 ; 26
  b. 28 ; 38
5a. Colour: 73 ; 74 ; 75 ; 76 ; 77 ; 91 ; 92 ; 93 ; 94 ; 95
  b. 97 ; 80
6a. 31   b. 32
7a. 77   b. 76

82 Reading Pictographs

1. 5   2. 55   3. March
4. April and May
5. February, because he had the fewest patients that month.
6. 300 ; 600 ; 350 ; 450
7. 2400   8. 250   9. 9

83 Making Pictographs

1.

2. Number of Gold Coins Collected
3. 10   4. 70   5. Uncle Jim
6. 20
7.

8. Number of Bags of Chocolate Eggs Sold
9. 350
10. 950
11. Sunday, because more people go shopping on Sunday.
12. 2150

84 Reading Bar Graphs

1. Number of Sandwiches Sold
2. Number of Sandwiches
3. Choice
4. 4 ; chicken breast, egg salad, corned beef, and turkey breast
5. 15   6. 50   7. 50 ; 40 ; 40 ; 20
8. Number of Storybooks Collected
9. Sean ; Mike   10. 70   11. 80
12. 150   13. 5

85 Making Bar Graphs

1.

2. Number of Children
3. spaghetti
4. 24
5. 80 ; 50 ; 30 ; 50

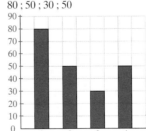

6. Number of Combos Sold   7. Combo
8. 130   9. 20   10. 210
11. Combo 3, because it is the least popular.

86 Circle Graphs

1. Kinds of Flowers Sold
2. 4 kinds ; carnation, rose, tulip, and chrysanthemum.
3. Rose
4. Tulip
5. Chrysanthemum
6. Tulip, because it is the least popular.
7.

8. 1
9. 4 ; 3 ; 1
10. Apollo
11. No, it would not be the same. He would be spending all his time on 'Apollo' and 'Lotus' because his assistant should be back in the office to work on 'A&B'.

87 Probability (1)

1a. 1, 2, 3, 4, 5, or 6
b. No
c. Yes
2a. A, B, C, D, E, or F
b. No
c. No
3a.
b.   c.
4a.
b. No   c.
5a.
b. No   c. No

88 Probability (2)

1. Likely   2. Likely   3. Unlikely
4. Certain   5. Impossible 6. Check b, d, and f.
7. B   8. Yes

89 Review

1. ; orientation ; pattern
2. ; position ; size
3.
4. 3
5. A ; B
6. ; quarter 7. ; half

8. Andrew's Savings

9. 160 ; 40   10. unlikely   11. impossible
12. likely   13. certain

90 You Deserve A Break!

1. Blocks Covered: D4, D5, E4, E5 ;

2. Blocks Covered: A1, A2, A3, B1, B2, B3, C1, C2, C3, D1, D2, D3 ;

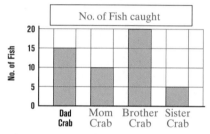

No. of Fish caught

3. Blocks Covered: G4, G5, G6, H4, H5, H6, I4, I5, I6 ;

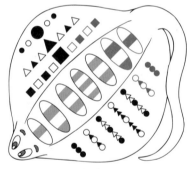

4. Blocks Covered: H1, H2, I1, I2, J1, J2 ;
   30 + 9 = 39 ; 31 + 9 = 40
5. Brother Crab
6. 50